With much ...
from

Shock
Amazement

Khandro Déchen
&
Ngakpa Chögyam

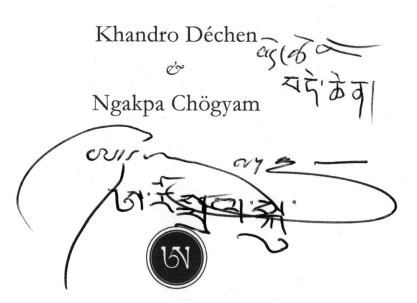

Aro Books worldwide

2018

Aro Books worldwide

PO Box 111
Aro Khalding Tsang
5 Court Close, Cardiff
CF14 1JR, Wales, UK

First Edition

ISBN 978-1-898185-45-1

aro-books-worldwide.org

We dedicate this book to:

Kyabjé Düd'jom Rinpoche Jig'drèl Yeshé Dorje

*Although Rinpoche passed into parinirvana in 1987—and
took incarnation in 1990—our memory of him has not faded
and his inspiration continues. He continues as
Kyabjé Düd'jom Sang-gyé Pema Shépa Rinpoche,
the second incarnation of Düd'jom Lingpa,
whose previous incarnations included Khyéchung Lotsa,
Mahasiddha Saraha, and Shariputra.*

Kyabjé Künzang Dorje Rinpoche

*Our Tsawa'i Lama and Heart Master who passed
into parinirvana in 2010 – our memory of
him remains as rich and vital as ever.*

*Both Lamas were Mahasiddhas, and it is to them that
we owe the greatest debt of gratitude in terms of
direct transmission of Dzogchen sem-dé
and Dzogchen men-ngag-dé.*

Without them, Shock Amazement *would have nothing
to offer but a skeleton-structure of information.
They were the living embodiments of Padmasambhava.*

Jomo Sam'phel Déchen

*The Sangyum of Kyabjé Künzang Dorje Rinpoche
remains with us as the continuing spacious inspiration
of the essential meaning of
what is conveyed in* Shock Amazement.
She is the living embodiment of Yeshé Tsogyel.

contents

Shock
Amazement

1

opening

The nomenclature *shock amazement*[1] is a description of a radical
state of being – the meaning of which will become clear as this
commentary proceeds.

Shock amazement also designates a practice: a practice that is
simple – yet, perhaps, too simple. Riding a horse is also simple,
unless it is found difficult. If it is found to be difficult, then the
explanation of a teacher will be necessary.

This work—entitled *Shock Amazement*—is an explanation which
addresses *that which is found to be difficult*. It is an instruction
guide to the *Aro naljor zhi*—the four naljors of Aro [2]—and to
the *Aro ting ngé 'dzin*[3]—the four absorptions of Aro. Although
these explanations relate to the Aro naljor zhi, the guidance
offered is not exclusive to that system.

---

1 Hèdéwa (*had de ba*), according to Dzogchen, has a range of meaning including:
shock amazement; surprised astonishment; astounded startlement; and, startled
awareness. It is sometimes used in a manner synonymous with mi-togpa (*mi rTog pa*)
—free of thoughts—and also, negatively (*outside the sphere of Dzogchen*), to refer to a
blank, dull state.
2 *A ro sems sDe rNal 'byor pa'i sNgon 'gro bZhi.*
3 *A ro sems sDe ting nge 'dzin bZhi.* See chapter 5.

It will therefore be found useful to anyone who engages in silent sitting practice.[4] Exercises will be given in a manner that can be followed – and advice given on the typical experiences which arise from following them.

It is assumed that readers will be conversant with basic Nyingma[5] Vajrayana[6] terminology – but footnotes are provided to ensure that readers understand the text.

Introduction to Dzogchen

Dzogchen[7] is the pinnacle of Vajrayana Buddhism. It is a cycle of teaching and of practices – but essentially Dzogchen is *the primordial condition of the individual.* It is thus both within and beyond the scope of conventional religion. As *the primordial condition of the individual,* Dzogchen is the state of referenceless relaxation in the vastness of each moment.

---

4 Other silent sitting systems include Formless Mahamudra (Chagya Chenpo Naljor Zhi / *phyag rGya chen po'i rNal 'byor bZhi,* Skt. catvari mahamudra yoga) of the Kagyüd School: one-pointedness (Tsé gÇig / *rTse gCig,* Skt. ekagrata); free of elaboration (Tro-dral / *sPros bral,* Skt. nisprapancha); one taste (ro gÇig / *ro gCig,* Skt. ekarasa); non-meditation (gom'mèd / *sGom 'med,* Skt. Abhavana), the state of integration with life.
5 Nyingma (*rNying ma*) is the oldest assemblage of lineages in Tibet. This Tradition pre-dates the schools of Tibetan Buddhism and has its source in the Buddhas Padmasambhava and Yeshé Tsogyel. Nyingma is a contraction of Nga'gyür Nyingma (*sNga 'gyur rNying ma*), which means the Ancient Translation Lineage.
6 Vajrayana – historically the vehicle of Buddhism subsequent to Mahayana. Vajrayana owes its origin to the secret teachings of Shakyamuni Buddha, given to the 84 mahasiddhas. These secret teachings, in turn, were absorbed by Padmasambhava who then taught Vajrayana in Tibet. Vajrayana contains both Tantra and Dzogchen. Tantra is the path of transformation and Dzogchen is the path of self-liberation. Self-liberation will be explained in chapter 5.
7 rDzogs pa chen po (*rDzogs chen / rDzogs pa chen po,* Skt. ati yoga or maha sandhi) – utter totality.

It is vast because it is undelineated by time. It is referenceless because the moment is experienced without allusion to past moments or future moments.

Dzogchen is the *self-existent confidence of being*[8] which arises spontaneously from beginninglessness. In terms of the experience of the path, the realised state—which is ever-present—*seems* to arise spontaneously.

It *seems* as if it were absent the moment before its appearance is recognised. With regard to practice, there is nothing to change – we simply need to relax.

Dzogchen is a system of nondual catalysts which self-describe the fundamental nature of *what we are* through *exploding the horizon of conventional reality.*

Dzogchen approaches our *essential nature* absolutely directly, but —because it is: too close, too accessible, too present, and too simple—it seems elusive.

Some have said that Dzogchen *stands alone* as a spiritual system – and, that it can be approached outside the context of Buddhist or Bön practice. Whilst it is true that Dzogchen has been practised by masters of all schools and traditions in Tibet, it is important however, to recognise that the *spiritual context of Tibetan culture* provided the religious framework from which it was approached. Lacking the spiritual culture which supports Vajrayana, this approach would present *perhaps* insurmountable difficulties for a Western practitioner. There have been masters of the Bön religion—such as Shardza Rinpoche[9]—who practised both Buddhist and Bön lineages of Dzogchen – but they were not separate from their spiritual background.

---

8 Rang-nè deng-chen (*Rang gNas gDeng chen*).
9 Shardza Tashi Gyaltsen (*shar rDza bKra shis rGyal mTshan*, 1859–1935).

5

There needs to be a realistic basis from which Dzogchen can be viewed as a possibility. It cannot merely be seen as an ultimate position from the standpoint even of well-intentioned intellectual zeal; this would have to be considered, even in the best possible light, as adolescent naïveté.

The Centrality of Lama and Lineage

Any teaching on Dzogchen will assume that people have engaged in the generation of compassion, the experience of silent sitting, and the development of devotion toward their Lama and lineage.

Those who attempt to practise Dzogchen *out of context* with the religious tradition that gave rise to it, often find themselves lacking the impetus to maintain regular practice.

Lacking the background of a religious context, people often find that the basic enthusiasm for *the discipline of meditation* dissipates. Certainly, without the richness and support of a religious tradition, it proves difficult to persevere through times when practice seems 'unrewarding'. From our experience, one has to belong somewhere. One has to be *part of something* which is *sufficiently larger than oneself*. To find support in a higher, deeper, broader context, one requires a context which goes beyond the isolated island of 'me and my process'.

Buddhism and Bön Vajrayana are the *religions of choice* for these practices – because Vajrayana is the sphere from which these practices originate. Those who consider themselves Nyingma practitioners will derive more inspiration from the *living colour* of these practices.

This is not a value judgement – merely a pragmatic statement designed to be helpful rather than to confine, alienate, or exclude. Inspiration is crucial to maintaining the practice of meditation; therefore there is a need to address the issue of how and from where inspiration is derived.

This book deals with Dzogchen sem-dé.[10] It contains material which requires transmission before it can be put into practice. We sincerely urge readers therefore, to seek transmission from a Lama.[11]

Dzogchen—the primordial state—is entirely accessible. Ironically however, it cannot be approached in isolation as an individual initiative. Committed preparation under the guidance of a Lama is necessary.[12] The Lama is indispensable. Similarly —although it is not entirely impossible to learn to ride a horse without an instructor—there are few who would be successful without the guidance of an experienced riding teacher. This— like all analogies—is flawed, because human beings are not *primordially qualified* to ride horses. The pragmatics of the analogy however, remain sound.

We speak from the basis of having studied and practised both equestrianism and Dzogchen – and we see many similarities in the value of studying and practising under experienced guidance. All human beings who endeavour to develop experience need to rely on those who have developed it before them.

---

10 *rDzogs chen sems sDe*. See chapter 2, footnote 23.

11 Readers would be advised to scrutinise the sophistry of those who claim that vajra commitment to the Lama is not a pre-requisite to Dzogchen. This will be clear to those who have received transmission – ka'bab (*bKa' babs*), and/or pointing-out instructions – ngo-trö nam (*ngo sProd rNams*).

12 See Ngakpa Chögyam, *Wearing the Body of Visions* (New York and London: Aro Books Inc, 1995).

This work is intended to provide practitioners with the necessary momentum to seek a Lama from whom direct guidance may be available. What we convey will be of value to that end, in laying the ground for what is to come – and in providing reference for those who have already received transmission.

2

naljor zhi

approaching the natural state

View, meditation, and action [1] are crucial to an understanding of Dzogchen.

View provokes or incites natural intelligence.
Meditation opens realisation to the view.
Action is the pure appropriateness or *spontaneity in the state of realisation.*

Action arises out of view and meditation – when they are realised—inseparably—as the spontaneous appropriateness of the nondual state. Most of what is contained within this book explores meditation, but that exploration will begin by examining *view.* View is both the collected experience of three thousand years of meditation practice – and the *natural uncreated logic* of reality. It could also be described as an array of glimmerings or glimpses of the nondual state – insofar as it can be pointed out [2] through oral, symbolic, and direct transmission.[3]

---

1 Tawa (*lTa ba*), gompa (*sGom pa*), and chopa (*mChod pa*).
2 Pointing-out instructions – ngo-trö nam (*ngo sProd rNams*).
3 The three styles of transmission as defined within the Dzogchen teachings are oral transmission (nyen gyüd/ *sNyan brGyud*); symbolic transmission (da gyüd/*brDa brGyud*), either formal symbolic (shèd lung da/*bShad lung brDa*) or informal symbolic (gyu-kyen da /*rGyu rKyen brDa*); and direct or mind-to-mind transmission (gong gyüd/*dGongs brGyud*).

View is pragmatic: when view is experientially integrated, it disappears. View then becomes personal knowledge.

This knowledge is similar to breathing – inasmuch as there need be no reminder concerning how to breathe: people simply breathe. View therefore, is a means of employing intellect to transcend intellect. To this end, view must always be tested in the laboratory of experience.

This is a creative use of intellect in which the *sensation of beingness* is confronted. Although intellect can be a masturbatory diversion from life, it *is* nevertheless, a genuine faculty – and can therefore become unentangled. An exploration of *being* entangled—and of how *being* becomes free from entanglement—is an essential precursor to Dzogchen.

To approach Dzogchen, it is vital to understand the meaning of self-liberation. According to the view of Dzogchen, the vehicles of Buddhism are divided into Sutra, Tantra, and Dzogchen.[4] Sutra is the path of renunciation.[5] Tantra is the path of transformation.[6] Dzogchen is the path of self-liberation.[7]

Sutra focuses on *the experience of emptiness*.[8] It therefore renounces addiction to form as a definition of being. It renounces attachment to reference points – and releases the need to protract a fixed perception of identity. Tantra focuses on the experience of *that which arises* from emptiness. It is based on the experience of emptiness and aims to realise the nondual nature of emptiness and form.

---

4 Sutra – Do (*mDo*), Tantra – Gyüd (*rGyud*), and Dzogchen (*rDzogs chen*).
5 Renunciation – ngé 'jung (*nges 'byung*).
6 Transformation – gyürwa (*sGyur ba*).
7 Self-liberation – rangdröl (*rang grol*).
8 Emptiness – tongpa nyid (*sTong pa nyid*).

It achieves this end through the transformation of that which is renounced by Sutra.

The transformation spoken of in Tantra addresses *the energy of dualism* – from the basis that this energy is simply a distortion of the nondual state. Dualistic derangements,[9] being, as they are, distortions of the nondual state, enable practitioners to recognise the nondual state through identifying—*one-pointedly*— with the fundamental energy of emotions.

Dzogchen is based on *the experience of nonduality* and actualises the nondual nature of emptiness and form – in every moment. It achieves this through naked observation – and concomitant nonreferential recognition of the self-liberating nature of arising form. That which is transformed through Tantra, is self-liberated through Dzogchen.

Self-liberation is not a term that describes itself without clarification – and to that end the Tibetan term will need to be explained. Self-liberation—in Tibetan—is rangdröl: *rang* means 'self', and *dröl* means 'liberation'. Self—as a translation of *rang* —is problematic in English, because it is not the same *self* as 'my *self*' or the mystical *self* spoken of in eternalist religious systems. It is more akin to the use of the word *self* as in *self-evident*. Thus, the *self* of rangdröl means *of-itself* and—by extension—*of-itself, it liberates itself.*

Nothing is renounced, as it is in Sutrayana – and nothing is transformed, as it is in Tantrayana. Whatever appears in terms of dualism is allowed to *liberate of-itself.*

There is therefore, no idea of liberation *for the self* or *by the self* – simply the natural propensity of everything that arises from emptiness to be undivided from emptiness.

---

9 Duality – nyi'dzin (*gNyis 'dzin*).

11

The dualistic predilection is to interfere referentially.

The word 'referentiality' refers to compulsive self-identification in terms of: employing the phenomenal world to prove that individual identity is solid, permanent, separate, continuous, and defined. This manipulative compulsion provokes constant attempts to make the world conform to the preferences prompted by conditioning.[10]

When allowing the emotional realm to be *as it is*, the freedom to experience the texture of life arises directly – and it becomes possible to sidestep the sour orthodoxy of preordained likes, dislikes, and habitual concepts.

Allowing perceptual life to be *as it is*, everything is self-liberated *as it is* – resulting in freedom from restrictive social rôles, conventional preoccupations, conservative anxieties, and mundane personal expectations.

Dzogchen speaks of the nonduality [11] of pattern and chaos.[12] It speaks of continuity and discontinuity [13] as being undivided.

This does *not* mean however, that there is no place for intelligent reasoning – but rather that the *unlearning process* is simply allowed to inaugurate itself. This is a process in which habits of compulsive attachment to conditioned patterns of intellect start to become transparent.[14]

---

10 Conditioning – gom'dri (*goms 'dri*).
11 Nonduality – nyi-su 'mèdpa'i dön (*gNyis su 'med pa'i don*).
12 Pattern and chaos – go-rim yöpa (*go rim yod pa*) and zing-zing po (*zing zing po*).
13 Continuity and discontinuity – kyé-wa'i gyün (*sKye ba'i rGyun*) and gyün-chèdpa (*rGyun chad pa*).
14 Transparent – zang-tal lé (*zang thal le*): the transparence of 'that which arises in Mind'.

The reach and range of reasoning-mind is small – and, although reasoning-mind is capable of remarkable feats, it cannot give us access to *all* the answers. Let us take an example. *Thinking* is not an effective means of dealing with emotional pain.[15]

Thinking *about* emotional pain invariably generates thoughts which run circles around themselves. Thinking never brings anyone nearer to an understanding of *what they are individually experiencing.*

Thinking *about* pain merely constitutes 'thinking around it' – *thinking about the circumstances which surround the pain.* People seldom think about *pain itself* – the reason being, that if they were to think about *pain itself*, they would unavoidably enter *the language of pain.* Thought is not capable of bringing us to an understanding of the fundamental texture of pain. Pain can only be *investigated* with the *non-conceptual observation* of meditation. Thoughts merely create a barrier – as if 'pain' and the 'experiencer of pain' were separate.

The way in which circular thoughts prevent sleep—even when the desire for sleep is ardent—will be familiar to many. Human beings are evidently addicted to the process of thought – and, as with any kind of addiction, there is a necessity to consider the consequences of 'the habit'. The next topic of exploration is the nature of 'the habit'.

---

15 See Ngakpa Chögyam and Khandro Déchen, *Spectrum of Ecstasy* (Shambhala Publications, 2002); and Ngakpa Chögyam, *Rainbow of Liberated Energy* (Element Books, 1984).

Sutra, Tantra, and Dzogchen

Preparation for Dzogchen is indispensable unless emptiness [16] has been experienced. Moreover, glimpses of the nondual nature of emptiness and form must also not be foreign. There are many approaches to the base of Dzogchen – but, simply stated, the fundamental ground of the Buddhist vehicles— Sutra and Tantra—must have been traversed.

There are many styles of riding a horse, and it may even be found that there is a natural mode which suggests itself of itself with each horse that is ridden.

But before such natural ease can be considered, it is indispensable to be able to walk, trot, canter and gallop— without falling—when circumstances cause the horse to stumble, swerve, or rear.

Suspicion—as to *the logistics of life*—is the basis for approaching Sutrayana. In order to become suspicious of *the logistics of life,* functional success needs to be achieved within the remit of dualism.

The term 'functional success' here simply refers to being a conventionally psychologically healthy adult, i.e., with the ability to carry out actions and plans – and take them to completion with competence. It does not refer to the acquisition of wealth or fame – it simply refers to capability.

Once functional success is achieved, the fact that it undermines itself in a predictable manner becomes increasingly evident with observation.

---

16 Emptiness here equates to the experience of mi -togpa (*mi-rTogpa*) – the absence of thought.

Firstly therefore, it is necessary to develop skills sufficient to the obtainment of desires. Such skills are developed through maintaining effort and continuing in a given direction.

If one gives up *(or fails to exert enough effort to obtain what is desired)*, then the point at which *suspicion of success* arises is never reached. With the obtainment of desire—either as possessions, circumstances, or associations—something unexpected occurs. This is often presented as *disappointment at the hollowness or worthlessness of desired objects* – but, whereas this is useful from a renunciate point of view, it does not address what Kyabjé Düd'jom Rinpoche describes as the *'infinite purity of the phenomenal world'*.[17]

According to the Dzogchen perspective—from which this quotation is derived—it is not seen as the fault of phenomena that satisfaction is not found in them.

Objects of desire are infinitely pure and entirely capable of providing enduring pleasure. The real problem lies with the fact that there is more interest in the process of acquisition than with the possessions, circumstances, or associations in themselves.

In the very moment of acquisition, the process that leads to acquisition – ends. Soon after the process ends, the experience of directionlessness begins. There is the sense of fulfilment— naturally—but that is undermined by the fact that there is no longer any engagement in the process of acquisition. *The process of acquisition* appears to provide a far stronger self-definition than *the state of having acquired*. When this is observed, motivation to question the situation arises.

---

17 From 'The Drinking Song of Kyabjé Düd'jom Rinpoche'. See Ngakpa Chögyam, *Wisdom Eccentrics* (Aro Books, 2011), page 482.

Suspicion and *questioning* occur simultaneously with glimpses of primordial nondual nature *(that continually sparkles through the fabric of conditioning).*

It is necessary to recapitulate at this point. Recognition of the *empty nature of being* is the basis for approaching Tantra. In order to enter the path of transformation it is necessary to see that *identity is momentary*. The 'I'—of what *I may be*—is only there, in the instant. This 'I' cannot be made into a project. A project is anything that extends 'I' beyond the moment. That is not to say however, that it is not possible to plan, in the ordinary sense of the word. It is simply not possible to plan as if this momentary 'I' were going to be present at some later point. The 'I' at the time of planning will no longer exist when the plan comes to fruition. No doubt the *'I' at the point of the culmination of the plan* may remember something of the *'I' who made the plan* – but the only connection is a series of reactions in time and space. As soon as the futility of turning 'I' into *an on-going project* becomes apparent – transformation becomes a startling reality.

Recognition of the nondual state is the basis for approaching Dzogchen – but, in order to enter the path of self-liberation, perceptual phenomena must come to be perceived from the experiential standpoint which is empty of references. It is only when the undivided nature of *that which arises* and *that from which phenomena arise* are first glimpsed that Dzogchen becomes feasible.

Before Dzogchen can be approached as a path – it stands to reason that the base from which Dzogchen practice commences has to have been reached.

In terms of experiencing the nondual base, this may initially consist of a series of brief flashes – but these fleeting experiences *must* occur, or the nature of the instructions for practice will seem incomprehensible.

Arrival at the base of any vehicle that is practised is indispensable – and there is no knowing how many years of preparation it may take to arrive at that ground of experience. It could be days or decades; there can be no fixed ordinance on the time required. For Dzogchen to become viable certain experiential criteria must be satisfied – otherwise *the methods that are called Dzogchen* will merely be *affectations that have the appearance of Dzogchen.*

Aro Naljor Zhi

Ngöndro—preliminary training—is required for every level of practice – *if* the requisite level, in terms of capacity, has not been reached. The capacity in question is that which would allow direct entry into the experiences indicated by the teaching. The word ngöndro [18] is used to describe many different practices – but it is important that the *Aro Sem-dé pa'i Ngöndro Zhi* not be confused with the Four Preliminaries of Tantra.[19]

The *Aro Sem-dé pa'i Ngöndro Zhi* is a cycle of teaching and practice from the Aro gTér lineage of the Nyingma Tradition. It is a small family lineage which originates with Khyungchen Aro Lingma [20] – a female visionary of the late 19th and early 20th centuries.

---

18 Ngöndro (*sNgon 'gro*).
19 Gyüdpa'i ngöndro zhi (*rGyud pa'i sNgon 'gro bZhi*). See Appendix I on the history of Dzogchen Sem-dé.
20 Khyungchen Aro Lingma (*Khyung chen A ro gLing ma*).

The Aro gTér was received in vision by Aro Lingma from Yeshé Tsogyel,[21] the female Buddha and consort of Padmasambhava.[22]

Although it places primacy on Dzogchen long-dé, the Aro gTér also places great emphasis on Dzogchen sem-dé – as this is the series which contains the approach to Dzogchen.

Dzogchen sem-dé is one of the *three series of Dzogchen*.[23] It is characterised as containing the most extensive body of teaching on conceptual mind *(sem)* and the nature of Mind (*sem-nyid)*. Dzogchen sem-dé is the series [24] which contains the most explanation, but that does not mean that it is intellectually communicable – unless the requisite experience exists. Although the three series of Dzogchen are non-hierarchic, sem-dé provides the entrance portal.

Sem-dé has sometimes been incorrectly translated as 'mental series' or 'mental class' by those unfamiliar with Dzogchen terminology – due to the fact that the word 'sem' literally means 'conceptual mind'.

Within the Dzogchen teaching however, 'sem' is employed as a contraction of the term 'sem-nyid'. Sem in Dzogchen terminology also relates to chang-chub-sem [25] or bodhicitta – the 'heart-mind of nonduality'.

---

21 Yeshé Tsogyel *(ye shes mTsho rGyal)*.
22 Padmasambhava *(Pad ma byung gNas)*, referred to in Tibetan culture as Guru Rinpoche.
23 Sem-dé *(sems sDe)*, the series of the nature of Mind; long-dé *(kLong sDe)*, the series of the vast expanse; and, men-ngag-dé *(man ngag sDe)*, the series of implicit instruction.
24 De *(sDe)*
25 Chang chub sem *(byang chub sems)*

As the ngöndro for Dzogchen sem-dé, the four naljors are the methods that enable the development of the necessary experiences through which Dzogchen becomes practicable.

The etymology of *naljor* is 'natural state – remaining'.[26]

So in ordinary contemporary English, the four naljors are: *the four methods of remaining in the natural state.*

The four naljors comprise the practices of shi-nè, lhatong, nyi'mèd, and lhundrüp.[27]

Shi-nè is presented here, sans preamble—because it is discussed in depth elsewhere.[28] Lhatong, nyi'mèd, and lhundrüp however, will require further introduction—with respect to *sem* and *sem-nyid*—before they will be found approachable.

Lhatong, nyi'mèd, and lhundrüp *can* be explained in fairly ordinary language – but that is no guarantee that the *meaning of the language* will be communicated. Some detailed background will therefore be indispensable.

This commentary on the Aro Naljor Zhi[29] is a practical investigation of the criteria which must be met in terms of the *experiential qualifications* of the individual. These *experiential qualifications* are not the creation of a spiritual culture – no matter how profound that culture. They are self-existent demands. If these self-existent demands are not met, the path is debarred *by the path itself.*

---

26 Naljor is a contraction of the words rNal ma – natural state, and 'byor pa – remaining. This word is used in Tantra to translate the Sanskrit word 'yoga' which means union, unifying, or unification. But in Dzogchen terminology the meaning relates to *remaining in the natural state.*

27 Shi-nè (*zhi gNas*), lhatong (*lha mThong*), nyi'mèd (*nyi 'med*), and lhundrüp (*lhun sGrub*).

28 See *Roaring Silence* by Ngakpa Chögyam and Khandro Déchen (Shambhala Publications, 2002).

29 Aro Naljor Zhi (*aro rNal 'byor bZhi*).

The self-existent demand of eating, for example, is that the mouth be opened. The self-existent demand of Dzogchen is equally as pragmatic.

Although preparation is required, there is no fixed 'conceptually based' law which can be applied, with regard to the exact nature of what brings a person to the base of the necessary experience – apart from devotion to the Lama.

Different traditions have different requirements of the individual – and it is therefore mandatory to request the advice of a Lama of the appropriate school or tradition. This book does not—and cannot—offer such advice or permission.

It is now salient to investigate the question of preparation. According to the Aro gTér, Dzogchen sem-dé [30] can be approached through its own unique ngöndro. Consequently, for those whose Lamas concur with this view, the sutric phase and the tantric phases [31] of kyé-rim and dzog-rim [32] are not mandatory. For those of other traditions however, the tantric ngöndro of the fourfold 100,000 practices [33] may be deemed indispensable before students approach Dzogchen.

Those who have Lamas from lineages where tantric ngöndro is deemed an indispensable prerequisite will need to receive dispensation from their own Lamas before proceeding.

---

30 Dzogchen sem-dé (*rDzogs chen sems sDe*).
31 Sutra covers the practices of emptiness and form with regard to renunciation and active compassion. Tantra covers the practices of purification and transformation.
32 sKyed rim and rDzogs rim are the 'generation' and 'completion' phases of Tantra. The generation phase deals with the envisionment of awareness beings (*wisdom beings or meditational deities*), and the completion phase deals with the practice of the spatial winds, spatial nerves, and spatial elemental essences.
33 The 100,000 prostrations with refuge and bodhicitta, the 100,000 mandala offerings, the 100,000 recitations of the Dorje Sempa 100-syllable mantra, and the 100,000 practices of Lama'i naljor or guru yoga.

Having stated that tantric ngöndro is *not* mandatory for the practice of Dzogchen sem-dé, it should be clearly understood that the result of tantric ngöndro is *always* necessary.

To practise Dzogchen, the base for its practice *has* to be established – by *whatever* means recommended and sanctioned by the specific preceptor Lama.

The phases of tantric ngöndro equate to traversing the levels of Sutra and Tantra with great swiftness. To be experientially equipped for the Dzogchen methods of *self-liberation*[34] this preparation cannot be omitted.

The four naljors, which prepare the ground for the practice of Dzogchen sem-dé in four ways, run parallel to tantric ngöndro in terms of their functional parameters. So whether practising according to one system or another – effective preparation is crucial.

The tantric ngöndro is the first stage of a symbolic method of arriving at the base of Dzogchen, and the four naljor ngöndro is a non-symbolic approach. Both approaches are characterised by the vehicle for which they are foundation practices. The tantric ngöndro has the *character of Tantra* and its innermost practice is the heart of Tantra. Likewise, the four naljor ngöndro has the *character of Dzogchen* and its innermost practice is the heart of sem-dé.

---

34 Rangdröl (*rang grol*) means self-liberation: 'of-itself it liberates itself ', i.e., the method is 'in-born' and 'self-accomplished' without the application of a method.

3

shi-nè

Shi-nè means *remaining uninvolved*. The literal meaning of shi-nè is *peaceful dwelling* or *calm abiding* – but these terms are not as pragmatically descriptive as *remaining uninvolved*. Shi-nè is the practice which undermines addictive referential attachment to the thought process. The word 'referential' describes the way in which phenomena—including conceptuality—are employed to prove that individual identity exists.

Shi-nè is a basic method of meditation which is also found in the other traditions of Tibetan practice.[1] Wherever it is taught however, it concerns the *relaxation of involvement with internal dialogue*. It concerns letting go of the mental gossip which inhibits direct perception. Shi-nè confronts the addiction to thought patterns.

Shi-nè provides face-to-face experience with: insecurity, fear, loneliness, vulnerability, and bewilderment.[2] These underlying tensions are common to all – and create distortion whether or not shi-nè is practised. Avoiding shi-nè is therefore not an answer. There is no choice in the situation. Whether the dualistic condition is acknowledged or not – it is what it is.

---

1 Shi-nè is found in all schools of Buddhism. In the 'Formless Mahamudra' of the Kagyüd School it is called tsé-gÇig (*tse gÇig*) – one-pointedness. In Zen Buddhism it is the initial phase of zazen.

2 The five adjectives relate—in order—to the five elements: earth, water, fire, air, and space.

It is better to understand it than to practise denial. Self-hidden vulnerabilities cause greater conflict in being hidden than in being exposed. Clarity spontaneously arises from the discovery of openness within the practice of shi-nè – and, once openness is discovered, the experience of the colour, tone, and texture of *thought* is also discovered. These qualities arise because sufficient experience of openness is developed in which thought is *seen* in a spatial context. Self-transparency manifests – and motivation becomes simpler in being seen nakedly. A natural compassion arises – a compassion which does not need to be forced or fabricated. This is the first real taste of freedom.

In order to understand the profundity of the relaxed approach of Dzogchen sem-dé, it is necessary to have direct experience of the fact that the mind cannot be forced. This is fortunately quite a simple discovery to make – and merely requires two sessions of practice.

First session

Sit in any position comfortable enough to maintain for two hours – and attempt, by any means at all, to force thought out of your mind.

Second session

Sit again in any position comfortable enough to maintain for two hours – and attempt to think continuously about anything at all. Let no gap occur in the flow of thought.

Explanation of the sessions

The result of the first session will be that thoughts increase as the tension of failure increases. A greater density of thought will be experienced than on other occasions where no force was employed.

The result of the second session will be that thought begins to evaporate after a fairly short period of time. It may even be the case that more gaps will have occurred—especially toward the end of the session—than will be experienced on other occasions where thought was merely dropped on observation. This is a traditional means of showing a student that *mind cannot be forced.*

Attempting to force thought out results in the proliferation of thought.

Attempting to force thought to be continuous results in the disintegration of the thought flow.

In a traditional setting, the result of the practice would not be explained – but Western audiences are not likely to follow such practices without explanation. In Tibet, much would have been made of the shock value of the experience – and perhaps the result would have been far more efficacious in terms of long-term understanding. In Tibet, the duration of the sessions would have required a full day—from dawn until dusk—but two sessions of two hours apiece will disclose a great deal.

It will show that: *To practise perfectly is to proceed without force. If the attempt is made to force thought out – the mind rebels. If the attempt is made to force thought to be continuous – the mind rebels.*

This is why, in the practice of shi-nè, thought is not encouraged – yet neither is it blocked. It is expedient now to introduce the adage: *Meditation* – isn't. *Getting used to* – is.

When it is said that '*Meditation* isn't' – it means that meditation is not *a method of doing*. It is a method of *not-doing*. There is no involvement in *doing* anything – there is simply the maintenance of *presence* in *motiveless observation*. When it is said that '*Getting used to* is' – it means simply *getting used to* – being. This requires acclimatisation to the undefined dimension of existence – *getting used to* being *referenceless.*[3]

In terms of acclimatising to the undefined dimension of existence – it should be understood that: imagination relies on empty perception; paintings rely on empty planes; sculptures rely on empty space; music relies on empty silent time; and, literature relies on empty conceptuality. If the art of freedom is to be realised—if creative potential is to be discovered—reliance on the experience of intrinsic emptiness is the only precursor.

The practice of shi-nè therefore, is the gateway to the *art of freedom* – but first it is necessary to disengage from the imagination – and cease to invent. Working with active imagination or envisionment[4] belongs to the sphere of Tantra. Although those tantric practices are extremely valuable, their principle and function is different from that of Dzogchen sem-dé.

Dzogchen sem-dé moves beyond emptiness and that which arises from emptiness into the sphere in which there is simply naked nature of perception – rigpa.

---

3 For what is meant by 'being referenceless', see below, pages 25-28.

4 See Ngakpa Chögyam, *Wearing the Body of Visions* (Aro Books Inc, 1995), chapter 4. Envisionment or visualisation is the practice of *internal seeing* in which there is identification with symbolic foci of realisation.

Rigpa [5] is naked perception [6] – a naked flame, which burns with or without fuel. It is naked in the same sense that the blade of an unsheathed knife is naked. Rigpa is pure and total presence. Stripped of referential clinging to the illusion of duality,[7] mind is self-divested through bare attention. The essential reality of what exposes itself, is simply *as it is*.[8]

The nature of *personal identified existence* needs to be mistrusted. The need to continually confirm personal identity seems hard-wired – because there is a continually observable engagement in the activity of seeking existential assurances. This is the dualistic penchant for unnecessarily clothing *naked awareness*[9] in concepts.

Nonduality is the state in which emptiness and form manifest as a seamless alternation in which each are aspects of the other – and have the same essential experiential flavour. Discussion of duality and nonduality—and the way in which duality is fabricated from the nondual ground of being—begins on page 29.

Mistrust of existence is the primary dualistic fixation – but it is a veiled mistrust which disguises itself as obduracy, irritation, obsessiveness, suspicion, and depression.[10]

---

5 Rigpa (*rig pa*) is a term which has a particular meaning in the Dzogchen teachings. It is employed in the other vehicles to mean 'knowledge' in the general sense of 'knowing about'. Within Dzogchen, rigpa is the term for the nondual state which is realised through methods of instant presence.

6 gÇèr-thong (*gCer mThong*).

7 Duality is the artificial separation and insularisation of emptiness and form.

8 'As it is' is the literal translation of the word chö (*chos*, Skt. dharma*)*.

9 Rigpa gÇèr-bu (*rig pa gCer bu*).

10 The five adjectives relate—in order—to the five elements: earth, water, fire, air, and space.

Because existence is mistrusted, the experience of being has to be continually scanned for *concretely viable* proofs. This mistrust of existence sets the scene for the manufacture of intermittent yet interminable struggle with the world.

Once struggle is underway: there must concomitantly be struggle with the outcome of that struggle, in order that the activity of *struggling* maintains itself. Without the practice of silent sitting, this kind of mistrust is never encountered face-on. If this experiential mistrust is never apprehended, the explanations presented in the following chapters will make little sense. It is therefore important to arrive at this level of understanding through the personal experience of practice.

Whilst practising shi-nè—when attention is found within *the gap which arises between thoughts*—the inclination is to fill such gaps with conceptual material in order to feel comfortable. Within these *gaps*, the inclination is to: grab the experience of *the gap*; to retreat from *the gap*; or to retract *presence* from *the gap*.

These three modes are termed attraction, aversion, and indifference. Whatever the mode of reaction however, the end result is the same: *the gap* is compulsively filled. Absence of thought is masked out. Whether self-referencing positively or negatively—or through the oblivion of neutrality—*the gap* is obliterated with concept. *Gaps* are filled with thoughts of acceptance or rejection – or attention drifts into vacancy. The tendency is to do anything rather than remain present in *the openness of being.*

Gaps of any kind—because they contain no confirmation of existence—are habitually filled. There is no intrinsic human trust in *beingness.*

Being is both: thought and absence of thought; phenomena and emptiness; pattern and chaos. When practising shi-nè however, it becomes evident that this existential definition is not comfortable to a dualistic mindset.

The practice of shi-nè allows the discovery of this existential definition to occur, at a pace which facilitates the assimilation and integration of these discoveries within an everyday perceptual context. Shi-nè practice shows that the dualistic system of self-referential proofs runs as follows:

In order to exist, 'I' have to know—all the time—that 'I' exist.

In order to be convinced of that knowledge, 'I' need constant proof of 'my' existence in terms of finding 'myself' to be: solid, permanent, separate, continuous, and defined.[11]

The discovery of shi-nè confronts fear of non-existence as being both the driving force of duality – and the *sparkling through* of nonduality. So—in one sense—it is quite justifiable to mistrust the nature of personal identity. That mistrust however, is usually aimed in the wrong direction. The open dimension of being is mistrusted rather than the conceptual criteria by which existence is habitually validated.

As soon as shi-nè is practised with sufficient determination, it is discovered that *definitions of existence* are a barrier to enjoying existence. The barrier is built of feelings of *insubstantiality, fear, isolation, agitation, and phlegmatic tedium.* Shi-nè is a provocative irritant to each of these feelings. Life also irritates these feelings – but not as definitively.

---

11 Solid, permanent, separate, continuous, and defined relate to: earth, water, fire, air, and space. See Ngakpa Chögyam with Khandro Déchen, *Spectrum of Ecstasy* (Shambhala, 2003). See also, Ngakpa Chögyam, *Wearing the Body of Visions* (Aro Books Inc, 1995).

As long as there is insistence on maintaining fixed definitions of personal identity, *the practice of shi-nè* and *life* will both appear to promote dualistic discomforts – and temporary dualistic remedies for them. Discomfort arises when definitions of existence dissolve – and temporary remedies to that discomfort are found in the arising of new definitions: thus the solution repeatedly becomes the problem.

The dualistic rationale continually seeks definitions – so, in a sense, shi-nè causes the relaxation of that continual struggle for self-definition.

Referentiality

The nature of existence continually helps and hinders the search for definitions in a completely impartial manner. This is self-evident once nonduality is understood even at the intellectual level, inasmuch as reality—being the nondual play of emptiness and form—will naturally appear to define everyone and everything, haphazardly, as either. Being applauded and reviled tend to alternate. The problem is the desire to be in charge of the defining process – as if dancing did not occur in terms of phenomena (*which continually appear both to provide definitions and to remove them*). This is a highly complicated procedure – but it is so customary, that it is hardly noticed. Rather than allowing continual re-definition (*and occasionally lack of definition*), the prevalent impetus is to attempt domination of the mutually defining and un-defining process which constitutes the flux of reality.

Control of this kind is unobtainable, because it would require that each individual existed as a fixed position within a fixed universe. Shi-nè threatens definitions whatever they are.

It reveals—either impishly or demonically—a strong belief in definitions. Shi-nè displays—either daintily or dreadfully—that dualistic mind thrives on definitions.

The phenomenal world is perfect, just as it is – but *diffidence, susceptibility, deficiency, mistakenness,* and *alienation* often characterise experience in uncomfortable alternation with *confidence, perspicacity, benevolence, accomplishment,* and *relaxed openness. Diffidence, susceptibility, deficiency, mistakenness,* and *alienation*—paired with *confidence, perspicacity, benevolence, accomplishment,* and *relaxed openness*—relate with the five elements: earth, water, fire, air, and space.

From the *perceptual stance* of shi-nè (*wordlessly observing the perceptual environment*), can it be said that the perceptual environment lacks anything? What should it *have* beyond what it *is*? Seeking for what might be lacking, can the nature of what is missing be elucidated? What should anyone have beyond what they *are*? What is this 'incompleteness'? How does this 'sense' arise—if no basis can be discovered—on which it could rest? These are peculiar questions – but they may shed further light on the meaning of the word Dzogchen as *uncreated self-existent completeness.*

Whether the sense of existence is complete or incomplete—fulfilling or unfulfilling—makes little difference in terms of Dzogchen. Dzogchen does not accept or reject the experience of either-or-both. At this point it would be prudent to examine what these ideas mean in the experience of the four naljors.

According to the Aro gTér,[12] referentiality is the process of *attaching to thoughts in order to provide proofs of existence.*

---

12 In respect of the Aro naljor zhi (*A ro rNal 'byor bZhi*), the four naljors of the Aro gTér (*A ro gTér*).

31

Referentiality is an unending unfulfilling process. The practice of shi-nè highlights the process of referential concretisation – and facilitates *seeing it for what it is.*

Reaching out for familiar patterns is the dualistic function which allows thoughts to serve as reference points. Thoughts, ideas, images, feelings, sensations, people, places, and things however, are not *reference points in themselves.* They are empty of referential qualities – but phenomena are reduced to reference points through the fear of loss of personal existence. The phenomena of the external world are thereby overlaid with secondary functions – attributed to them for dualistic convenience. The messages that are imagined as being received from the phenomenal world are *attributed* rather than *inherently provided.*

It is no different with the phenomena of human psychology. With psychological patterning however, it is only possible to make the *discovery of attribution* through the practice of shi-nè. When sitting in silence – it is discovered that the *secondary function of thought* is to prove the reality of existence.

Without thoughts there are no reference points. Without thoughts there is nothing to validate the experiential qualities of being as solid, permanent, separate, continuous, and defined. Shi-nè is *getting used to* that. In everyday life, the continual search for reference points distorts experience. It makes experience appear to be unsatisfactory.

Although the sensation of unsatisfactoriness is irritating or torturous, it appears to be endurable – in that it satisfies the need for self-definition.

This is what makes it possible to be distracted from *being* through continual *attempts to be* – and this 'attempting to be' is manufactured by 'doing': 'attempting to *be* solid' is acted out; 'attempting to *be* permanent' is acted out; 'attempting to *be* separate' is acted out; 'attempting to *be* continuous' is acted out; and, 'attempting to *be* defined' is acted out. This 'acting out' style designs itself on the basis of dualism.

This basic misconception is that it is only the *form qualities of being* which have the capacity to validate existence. Dualistic vision takes 'existence' and 'non-existence' to be mutually exclusive – and in so doing, strays into unending cycles of dissatisfaction. Through grading what is perceived in terms of *reference value*, only three responses are available: attraction, aversion, and indifference.

If what is perceived substantiates personal definitions, *attraction arises*.

If personal definitions are threatened, *aversion manifests*.

If the phenomena of perception neither substantiate nor threaten personal definitions, *there is indifference*.

What cannot be manipulated referentially is ignored. Phenomena are rarely experienced *as they are*. Experience is limited according to the need for definitions – and consequently everything is graded as to its suitability as a possible reference point.

There is nothing wrong with *thought* – even though some categories of meditation instruction would have you accept that this is the case. According to Dzogchen, *thought is a natural function of Mind* – and, just as the other sense faculties are *natural* to physical existence, so too is thought.

Moreover, thought—according to Buddhism in general—is a sense-faculty, rather than a function that is separate from the senses.

Finding Mind to be a referenceless ocean of space allows the dualistic knot of panic to untie itself. In experiencing this space, a brilliant discovery is made: *being referenceless* is not death. If immanent incidence [13] can be maintained in *natural uncontrived presence*—without sinking into oblivious drowse—spontaneous clarity is disinhibited. Stars appear in the sky and their brilliance is reflected in the referenceless ocean of being.

Explanations such as this can either be understood on the basis of immediate recognition—which originates in practice—or from the *sparkling through* of the nondual state. Explanations such as these are springboards for the discussion of referencelessness. Such springboards are built of *ideas designed to undermine ideas.* They are intended to enable a *leap into the space of referencelessness* – a plunge into an understanding of *the vastness of being.*

Conventional Logic and Realised Reasoning

At this point it is salient to introduce two terms that may be helpful in relating to the ways in which different kinds of information can be assimilated: these terms are 'conventional logic' and 'realised reasoning'. *Conventional logic* is what is regarded in the world as being acceptable as logic.

Realised reasoning is based on experience which lies outside the realm of conventional logic – because it is based on experience that lies outside what is conventionally understood in terms of human experience.

---

13 Rang ché su yödpa (*rang chas su yod pa*) – immanent incidence, intrinsic, present as an innate quality, natural possession; inherently present as a natural attribute of being.

There is no way in which the realm of realised reasoning can be approached with the battering ram of conventional logic. All that can be ventured is enquiry as to how to accomplish the arrival at this level of experience *(from which it becomes possible to relate to realised reasoning).* The answer to this question is made up of methods: the first is the practice of shi-nè.

Once having gained some experience of sitting, openness to the stream of realised reasoning bases itself on the field of experience which has been entered.

Once open to realised reasoning, encouragement to bring everything to the level of practice is natural. The further the practice of sitting is taken, the more open the situation becomes. The faculties become less limited by conventional logic. Barriers dissolve between the boundaries of understanding and the wider horizons of realised reasoning – which were formerly found to be frustrating.

Divorced Individuation and Nonduality

The practice of shi-nè eventually develops into further practices in which horizons of experience open into vivid displays of integration. Shi-nè is the gateway to the experiential freedom in which *individuation* and *oceanic experience* are not mutually exclusive. The traditional analogy is of a fish within an ocean.

When *fish and ocean*[14] begin to *participate in each other* – it is realised that many seeming polarities of experience are simply ornaments of the nondual state. Nondual realisation is possible at any moment. The intrinsic spaciousness of being is a continuous reminder to us of *nondual beingness.*

---

14 Nya dang gyamtso (*nya dang rGya mTsho*).

Living as if divorce were possible—in terms of individuation and oceanic experience—is a disconnected perspective that could be termed *divorced individuation*. From this dualistic perspective, reminders of nondual being-ness are interpreted as a threat to existence. Divorced individuation creates the illusion that fixed definitions—unsteady as they may be—remain viable. The illusion flickers like an old motion picture – but it is possible to catch glimpses of the white screen. The glimpses are conveniently blurred however – and the flickering frames melt into each other. There is an unspoken agreement to avoid suspecting that the *images seen* are *not* really there.

The idea is that the audience forgets that they are watching an intangible image projected onto a screen. There is an illusion of solidity, permanence, separation, continuity, and definition – and the audience relates to that as being real.

When watching a film, the audience has to pretend that it is real in order to enjoy the film. This—in the language of drama—is called 'willing suspension of disbelief '. With regard to the *sense of being* however, 'willing suspension of disbelief' is an actively determined—continuously prolonged—withdrawal of disbelief.

The world of perception teeters precariously between existence and non-existence. From the perspective of *conventional filtered vision*, the phenomena of perception are seductive, provocative, and highly misleading. Substantiality and insubstantiality dance together. It could resemble a fan dance in which the ostrich-plumes of emptiness and phenomena occlude reality, whilst simultaneously being none other than the *voluptuousness of being* that is being titillatingly occluded. Although, somehow, there *is* something else – but it can only be *seen* if occasionally meditation dispenses with the duality of the fans.

The *naked lady of nonduality* [15] is only occluded fleetingly by the *flickering feathers* of the *ostrich-plume fans*. Unless *this* is understood, it is impossible to *see* what is happening. Unless it is realised that both the *lady* and her *fans* are equally *naked* and equally *delightful*, [16] nothing is perceived other than form – and that *form* is neither the lady nor her fans. It is merely an assemblage of visual coordinates upon which conceptual constructs can be erected.

Maintenance of the illusion of being *solid, permanent, separate, continuous,* and *defined* is only necessary because the sense of divorced individuation requires it for its putative survival.

In order for *individuated existential identity* to experience itself as *solid, permanent, separate, continuous* and *defined*, identification is necessitated in relation to facets of phenomena which temporarily display those qualities.

The struggle required to maintain this illusion stems from the fact that nonduality *sparkles through* the fabric of duality – and this sparkling continually undermines dualistic attempts at manipulations.

Being is continually poised on the brink of effortlessness – but continually creates distractions in order to sustain the sense of divorced individuation. These delirious, distressing, and dreary deviations from effortlessness are the mechanisms employed to maintain the illusion of duality.

---

15 Female gender is used because the nondual state is called Küntuzangmo (*kun tu bZang mo*, Skt. Samantabadri – total wholesomeness) in the Aro gTér lineage. Küntuzangmo is also depicted as the dharmakaya form according to the Tröma Nakmo drübthab of the Düd'jom gTér-sar cycle. Küntuzangmo is the female equivalent to Küntuzangpo (*kun tu bZang po*) more generally used in the Nyingma tradition. Künzang Yab-yum (*Küntuzangmo and Küntuzangpo in sexual union*) is an anthropomorphic representation of the nondual state.

16 Nakedness – gÇer-bu (*gCer bu*) and delight – kuntu ga' (*kun tu dGa'*) equate with emptiness and form.

These mechanisms are constantly under threat of *disillusionment*. Disillusionment is the continuous *nondual intimidation* offered by the *nature of reality itself* – and, from the experience of this 'intimidation', there arises a specific kind of dualistic self-protective activity. This activity consists of *generating commitment to fleeting apparitions of stability*. This is the character of duality.

Nonduality, on the other hand, is completely relaxed in the flow of *whatever is*. It could be said that if all phenomena had the duration of mere minutes *(if everything changed erratically everywhere)* dualism might not be able to maintain itself.

Nothing that comes into existence has the *qualities* of *solidity, permanence, separateness, continuity,* or *definition.* These qualities can never be found as fixed features of anything – yet, everything shares these *qualities* temporarily.

Because everything shares these qualities on a temporary basis, it becomes possible to generate illusory versions of reality.

These versions of reality however, are simply further fan-dances – where the ostrich-plumes are either: substantiality and insubstantiality; permanence and impermanence; separateness and indivisibility; continuity and discontinuity; or definition and indefinability.

These fan-dances, from the nondual perspective, are not samsara. Nor are they nirvana. They are therefore beyond illusion. They are ornaments of *sheer naked presence.*[17]

---

17 Jèn-nè çér-ré-wa (*rJen ne cer re ba*) – alternatively, rang-ngé jènpa'i yeshé (*rang gnas rjen pa'i ye shes*).

Time without Content

This is the conclusion of the practice of shi-nè – but not the conclusion of practice. Shi-nè expedites experience of time without content – mind sans mental-events. The purpose of shi-nè is to facilitate experience of Mind in which referencelessness is discovered. This is the realisation of emptiness – and the knowledge that thoughts or mental-events are not in themselves the *fabric of Mind*. The *nature of Mind* is sheer brilliant emptiness. The *instruction/direction*—at this stage of practice—is to remain in this *empty state* and to enter into what is known as stabilised shi-nè.

Stabilised shi-nè [18] is a condition of mind in which mental events no longer arise for substantial periods within sitting sessions. Having reached the stage of *simply continuing* – the neurotic desire to generate thoughts in order to establish reference points is momentarily exhausted.

As soon as shi-nè is stabilised, a new challenge needs to be faced. At this point a potential problem can manifest – and will need to be resolved if practice is to continue to develop.

This problem is termed sleepy shi-nè.[19] It is a state in which mental events are absent, but in which *presence of awareness* is also absent. It is at this point that shinè needs to be dissolved, by entering into lhatong. Lhatong means 'further vision' and represents the way beyond emptiness – which is the beginning of the journey into vastness.

---

18 Shi-nè kyi ting'dzin (*zhi gNas kyi ting 'dzin*) is also known as stable shi-nè. This should not be confounded with shi-nè 'gogpa (*zhi gNas 'gog pa*) – shi-nè of cessation, which is the result of regarding meditation practice as being the act of cultivating and fixating on a state in which sensations and thoughts are absent. This is a sidetrack which does not lead to the nondual state.

19 Sleepy or lethargic shi-nè – shi-nè tengpo (*zhi gNas lteng po*).

4

lhatong, nyi'mèd, and lhundrüp

The state of referencelessness may seem ineffable when
discussed in the context of Vajrayana – but it is not a rarefied
state.

Oceans are referenceless if their boundaries cannot be
distinguished. The sun by day—and the moon and stars by
night—allow navigation – but there is no intention or design
behind these appearances. The ocean of Mind is referenceless
– yet the play of Mind-phenomena allows *conceptual navigation*.
There is however, no intention or design beyond the energetic
play of that which arises within Mind. Concepts arise in
random-order; in arbitrary-pattern – and as Mind-phenomena
they are simply an aspect of the vivid displays of *primordial
compassion*.[1]

In the previous chapter we explored the *currents which animate
the surface of the ocean of Mind*. We explored the need to define
beingness as solid, permanent, separate, continuous, and
defined. Now we can consider the possibility of *gazing* at the
glittering surface of this ocean of Mind – at sun-light and
star-light glinting.

---

1 Yé-zhi nyingpo changchub kyi sem (*ye gZhi sNying po byang chub kyi sems*). Also,
lodral jenpa'i rang zhal (*bLo bral rJen pa'i rang zhal*) – the primordial bodhicitta of the
primordial state.

Gazing[2] is an openness which sees—with *transparence*[3]— the nature of our relationship with reference points.

Dualistic reactions to *sheer naked presence*[4] of the nondual state cause convoluted contrivances to play themselves out as the dualistic texture of life experience. We therefore act as if there were no connection between *what we are* and *where we are* – as if there were no connection between 'I' and what this 'I' has come to describe as 'the external world'.

This dualistic speculation propounds a philosophy in which connections are made or broken on the basis of pre-conditioned choices – *as if* we were completely free to insulate ourselves from whatever we regarded as uncomfortable. In terms of the experience of existence, this dualistic philosophy often collides painfully with the *natural philosophy* of reality.

Within this free condition—of the *natural philosophy* of reality—everything subtly affects and changes everything else. It is therefore not possible to set up a 'private reality' without creating a staggering array of absurdly unworkable complexities. Any attempt to *insularise* areas of interest or involvement is always subject to the continuing modifications that are outside our control. There are: no static objects; no static situations; no static beings; and, no static life.

The fabric of existence is a *fluxing web*[5] or 'magical manifestation web' of infinite dimensions.

---

2 Gazing with wide, tranquil, awakened eyes – hur ga-tu zig (*hur bGa tu gZigs*). Alternatively, thong-ngo (*mthong ngo*) or gyang-so tépa (*rGyang so blTas pa*).
3 Zang-thal (*zang thal*).
4 Rig pa'i tsal (*rig pa'i rTsal*).
5 Kun-trol (*kun khrol*) – describes an infinite series of patterns which arise and dissolve into each other. Kun-trol is not a *philosophically monist* fixed design. With regard to Buddhist nonduality, form is necessarily empty and therefore no fixed pattern can ever be held to have permanent existence.

Existence is a *fluxing* web whose threads are the energy of form and emptiness – of existence and non-existence.

The style or pattern of individual existence sets up tremors in the web of which individual existence is a part. The tensions of the threads alter – and every part of the web is affected. One cannot 'enact' without affecting everything and, at the same time, being affected *by* everything. Pattern affects pattern, creating further pattern. Pattern evolves out of chaos and becomes chaos again. Pattern and randomness dance together: ripples in water extend and collide with other extending ripples; a fish leaps to catch an insect; a wild goose takes to the sky; the wind blows; and, a child throws a pebble into the lake. Nothing in this *fluxing web* happens in isolation. Isolation is not possible. We cannot isolate what we are from what we conceive of as the external world. We are part of an ocean in which *fish* and *water* participate with each other – in which *fish* without *water* is as untenable as *water* without *fish*.

Beyond the experience of emptiness [6] is the experience of how *energy* manifests as the endless display of Mind. [7]

It is often imagined that the final goal of practice is to attain a condition of mind in which thought has been entirely abandoned. It is not surprising that this idea exists – because many forms of meditation instruction deal with the *stabilisation of shi-nè*, in which emptiness is the goal. It is not unusual therefore, that little emphasis is given in such teachings as to what lies beyond emptiness.

---

6 Mi-togpa *(mi togs pa)*, the state of no content of mind, no mental manifestations, no namthogs *(see footnote 11, below)*.

7 Sem-nyid *(sems nyid)* – the *nature of Mind*, in distinction to sem *(sems)* – conceptual mind, which arises within the expanse of Mind. See chapter 2, naljor zhi, page 14.

43

There is nothing false with regard to explanations which posit emptiness as the fruit – and those who explain in this way are perfectly correct according to the view of the specific practices they describe.[8] According to many teachings within the sutras, emptiness *is* the goal.

Dzogchen however, requires subtlety and precision with regard to *how* emptiness is defined as being *an aspect of the goal*. This is not particularly controversial, because the Heart Sutra states quite succinctly that

'... *form is emptiness and emptiness is form.*'[9]

The aspect of Sutra[10] which equates with *form* is compassionate activity. Form is never seen as separable from *emptiness* within the nondual state. Therefore *emptiness* must ultimately be considered both in terms of dualistic and nondual experience. If *emptiness* and *form* are nondual, then the experience of *emptiness* must relate with the unimpeded arising and dissolving of *form*. From this perspective, emptiness without relation to form could simply be the most rarefied manifestation of dualism.

Let us examine the matter in closer detail. Emptiness is the fruit of the practice of shi-nè. The end result of this practice is the absence of namthogs[11] – arising thought.

---

8 Teachings are given according to specific yanas or vehicles, and these teachings differ in their emphasis according to the principle of the particular path.

9 The Heart Sutra, Nying mDo (*sNying mDo*). Chomden Déma Shérab Rabkyi Pharoltu Jinpa'i Nyingpo (*bCom lDan 'das ma shes rab kyi pha rol tu phyin pa'i sNying po*), the Bhagavati Prajnaparamita Hridaya Sutra. See Appendix II – translation of the Heart Sutra.

10 In the context of this book Sutra equates with shravakayana, pratyékabuddhayana, and bodhisattvayana. Sutra is then viewed as the first of three vehicles: Sutra, Tantra, and Dzogchen.

11 Namthog (*rNam rTog*) means that which arises in Mind. Namthogs can be anything; not simply thought – but patterns, colours, textures, and feelings.

Although the absence of namthogs is the end result of shi-nè, it is not the end of practice, or of realisation. There are further stages of practice – and these deal with the energies which continually manifest as the *natural function of emptiness*. These also deal with the reintegration of energy with the *presence of awareness*.

The discovery of emptiness is a stage in the process of realising the beginningless nondual state. So, if we become fixated with the idea of resting in the space of *Mind without content*, it becomes a spiritual cul-de-sac.

Mind without thought is a condition which is as unnatural as *Mind occluded by thought*. So why proceed thus far, merely to experience another limited state of being? In order to answer this question we need to explore further – and ask what *Mind* is taken to be.

Without meditative experience, even examination or investigation of conceptual mind would be limited. So if we looked at the *nature of Mind* in the usual way we examine phenomena—in order to elucidate their nature—we would merely find *mental events*. We would be confronted with thoughts: the very thoughts which constituted the method of observation – as well as the subject those thoughts had observed.

Observing *Mind* in this way would merely reveal an endless series of thoughts – and this self-limiting activity would never uncover the *nature of Mind*: it would just ensnare us in an intellectual kaleidoscope, which we would doom ourselves to revolve incessantly.

Unfortunately that would be the end of the quest whether we realised it or not. It would be imagined that Mind *was* thought – and that would be the end of the exploration.

45

Examining the nature of Mind-phenomena—employing thought as a tool—would limit the character of the thought-structures at our disposal. Thought would be examining thought with thought – which would become incrementally ludicrous. The *thoughts* with which *thoughts* were examined would have to be examined – and what would examine those thoughts apart from thought (*which would also need to be examined*)?

Thought cannot examine itself in any ultimate sense – it is a closed system. Thought can no more examine its own nature than a knife cut itself, or an eye see itself. The only way an eye can see itself is to avail itself of a mirror. The nature of that mirror—vis-à-vis *thought*—is the natural reflective capacity of Mind, which is beyond thought. To investigate the nature of thought – we need to use some capacity *other* than thought. In order to discover what other means there are at our disposal to investigate *the nature of thought* we need to detach from obsessive relationship with thought.

So shi-nè—the practice of remaining uninvolved with thought—is the starting point.

In the practice of shi-nè, practice-time is utilised in *letting go* and *letting be*. Through *letting go* and *letting be* it becomes possible to witness the fact that Mind is not merely thought. When first looking at Mind—without the practice of thought-free observation—all that is seen is the two-dimensional screen of thought.

We therefore take mind to be thought – and René Descartes posited his existence on that basis.[12] Buddhism would naturally take this assertion further—maybe in three stages: *I think therefore I think; I think therefore thinking occurs;* and simply, *thinking.* Thinking does not prove there is a thinker – or rather an *underlying thinker* or *overarching thinker* who gives rise to thoughts. Thinking does not prove that there is continuity in terms of that which gives rise to thought.

Mind is misunderstood as a patchwork or a pastiche of interlocking, overlapping thought. It is as if one were looking at the surface of a lake ruffled by the wind, or the sky churning with clouds. From these impressions, no one would evolve the notion that the surface of the lake could be like a mirror perfectly reflecting the sky. No one would have any idea that behind the clouds lay the infinity in which the sun shone or the moon and stars glittered within the vastness of space. If one rigged up a wind generator in order to examine the lake, one would merely create more disturbance – and all one would learn would be that waves can become more pronounced. One would gain no idea of the natural reflective capacity of the lake. If one set up a gigantic cauldron which issued up yet more water vapour into an already overcast sky – one would not be likely to get any insight into the nature of the sky, with regard to its capacity to manifest clouds.

---

12 Cogito ergo sum: I think therefore I am. This is the philosophical proposition made famous by René Descartes. The simple meaning of the Latin phrase is that thinking about one's existence proves—in and of itself—that an 'I' exists which thinks. René Descartes explained, '*We cannot doubt our existence while we doubt.*' This proposition became a fundamental element of Western philosophy, as it was perceived to form a foundation for all knowledge. While other knowledge could be a figment of the imagination, a deception, or a mistake, the very act of doubting one's existence was argued as providing proof of the reality of one's existence.

When involvement with thought is retracted however, the turbulence diminishes – the cloud-cover attenuates. The wind subsides and we begin to see reflections on the surface of the lake. Occasional gusts may ruffle the surface again – but we know that water is not always in motion; sometimes it is still.

When thought ceases to be generated as an obsessive process, the clouds begin to dissipate – and occasional shafts of sunlight strike through – and intermittent traces of blue are witnessed. As soon as it is understood that the *two-dimensional screen of thought* is a construction, we can commence to inaugurate the process of discovering emptiness. Once emptiness is revealed, the concomitant discovery is that *existence without reference points* is possible. This proceeds to the discovery that there is a natural relationship between emptiness and the spontaneously manifesting energy of emptiness.

The free nature of Mind is neither a flat screen of thought, nor a void in which nothing occurs. Both are partial conditions – but, once we have learnt that we can let go of thought, we can open up to a more fluid, frictionless, non-adhesive relationship with thought.

It may come as a surprise that *thought is not antithetical to the nondual state*. Often when meditation is discussed, the main emphasis is given to the abolition of thought. Many practitioners therefore, come to the conclusion that thought itself is the enemy. Thought however, is a natural function of Mind. Where nothing arises from emptiness, there is no energy – and, consequently, no clarity.[13]

---

13 Within the Dzogchen tradition, the natural movement of namthogs within the space of Mind is known as sèl (*gSal*) clarity.

The reason for continuing in practice in order to arrive at a *state without thought* is that it provides the space to unlearn the neurotic relationship with thought.

Lhatong

If we return to the idea: *meditation* – isn't, *getting used to* – is, we can see that the process, or *space of unlearning,* is *getting used to* the referenceless quality of being. Letting go of neurotic involvement with thought can be looked at in a similar way to letting go of a drinking problem. If one wishes to overcome alcoholism, one may well have to desist from drinking for a protracted period. If however, it never becomes safe to drink again—without the fear of returning to alcoholism—one cannot say that one is no longer an alcoholic: one has simply become an abstemious alcoholic.

The time spent resisting the inclination to become inebriated—and time undergone without the sense of deprivation—are significant to the learning process. Time is deployed—in this case—to prove that alcohol is not needed in order to live. Once there is the certainty that drunkenness is no longer a refuge, one can drink and see what happens.[14] If the immediate impulse is to drink compulsively, one knows that one is still alcoholic. If one or two glasses suffice however, one is free to have a drink whenever it is appropriate. So it is with everything – with thought and with all phenomena.

When we can enter into a condition without thought and remain *present* and *awake* in that experience for extended periods of time – we know that the relationship with thought has undergone a radical change.

---

14 This analogy of alcoholism, whilst being accurate according to the meditative process, is not recommended for anyone who is or has been an alcoholic.

This is stabilised shi-nè – and once we have established this practice, we can dissolve shi-nè and enter into the practice of *lhatong*.

The dissolution of shi-nè can seem to be the defeat of everything one has sat so long to accomplish – but it is a vital part of the process if one is interested in continuing the journey into vastness.

Unless shi-nè is dissolved there is a possibility of becoming addicted to absence.

Practitioners who simply remain with 'absence of thought' become *absence-addicts* rather than *thought-addicts*.

It is difficult to remain for long in stabilised shi-nè without drifting into sleepy shi-nè. It is comforting to dwell in the condition of sleepy shi-nè and—from the initial standpoint of never having practised—it could appear to be an accomplishment.

The danger of sleepy shi-nè is that—lacking this admonition— one might take this state to be the end result of practice. So, once stable shi-nè becomes a reliable phase of meditation, we need to dissolve shi-nè. In order to dissolve shi-nè, we have to allow namthogs to re-emerge – but not by re-engaging in the neurotic process of generating reference points.

When we dissolve shi-nè—and allow the natural energy of Mind to re-emerge from emptiness—we are not *creating* anything – we are simply *allowing*. As soon as energy begins to re-emerge, all that is necessary is to allow that energy the freedom to manifest.

One then finds presence of awareness both in the emergence of that energy from emptiness – and its dissolution into emptiness. This type of experience is likened to *the leaping of fish from the still surface of a lake.*

When fabulous fish leap into existence from nothingness—exploding the mirror surface of the lake—there are three vital considerations: the still lake; the leaping fish; and, the awareness which is present in both.

The still lake is emptiness, or the absence of namthogs. There is nothing there but *presence.* This is the discovery of shi-nè.

The leaping fish, or arising namthogs *(texture/colour/pattern/ thought/sensation)*, move without referential co-ordinates. This is the discovery of lhatong.

Initially this practice of dissolving shi-nè and wordlessly observing the fish jumping from the still lake is known as lhatong. Lhatong means 'further vision'. It is an extraordinarily vivid experience. It is vivid because—for the first time—thought is no longer experienced as two-dimensional. Mind is no longer a flat screen comprising overlapping interlocking thought sequences. Namthogs now arise in a spatial context. Lhatong allows the experience of colour, texture, and tone. With the practice of lhatong, we find the presence of awareness in the movement of the energy which arises from the empty state.

Within this spaciousness we can ultimately find moments of *instant presence*, or nondual recognition of being.[15] In this way, the movement of arising and dissolving namthogs becomes the nature of the path.

---

15 'Instant presence' is one of a number of ways in which *rigpa* can be translated. There is also nondual awareness, presence of awareness, and nondual presence.

One method of allowing fish to jump is to open the eyes completely. Having opened the eyes – the immediate tendency is to grasp at thoughts. At this point frustration is probable. To open the eyes and find the presence of awareness in whatever arises, is a simple instruction – but it is not necessarily easy to follow.

This movement of namthogs—this jumping of the fish from the clear lake of stabilised shi-nè—is called *gYo-wa*.[16] gYo-wa means 'movement' – and it is in this movement that the presence of awareness must be found (*rather than losing presence through attachment to the intellectual content of the moving namthogs*). No comment is made on the namthogs. There are no judgements as to whether the jumping fish are beautiful or grotesque – presence of awareness is simply found in their movement. One allows oneself to become identified with *that which moves.*

Having reached this point, we now need to return in our discussion to the nature of practice.

Whilst engaging in the practice of lhatong, distraction or problems of lack of presence can be mediated by techniques. There are specific methods which relate directly with the functioning of energy at the levels of *mind, voice,* and *body.*

In the following pages there are three exercises which work with energetic imbalances – and they will prove helpful at this stage of practice. We have outlined the primary practice according to the system of shi-nè and lhatong – so now, it is important to become familiar with their complementary methodology.

These auxiliary practices—belonging to the categories of *mind, voice,* and *body*—relate to the three spheres of being.

---

16 gYo-wa (*gYo ba*).

These are *chö-ku, long-ku* and *trül-ku.*[17] Chö-ku is the sphere of unconditioned potentiality – the dimension of emptiness. Long-ku is the sphere of intangible appearance – the dimension of energy *(the infinite display of light and sound)*. Trül-ku is the sphere of realised manifestation – the dimension of physicality.[18] Whatever problem of distractedness arises, one begins at the level of mind. If that proves ineffective, one moves to the level of voice. If that is fruitless, one moves to the level of body. The three exercises which follow are practices of *mind, voice,* and *body* and should be practised in that sequence.

---

17 Chö-ku *(chos sKu)*, long-ku *(longs sKu)*, and trül-ku *(sPrul sKu)*.
18 A realised human being *(tülku)*, or a realised being in other locations or dimensions.

One: *the practice of mind*

Sit in a posture of comfort and alertness. Relax the eyelids so that they are lowered to a point where they are partially open – sufficient only to let in light. This relaxed position prevents the eyes from flicking. The Tibetan letter 'A' (*pronounced 'ah'*) is visualised as shown.

The letter 'A' is white and composed of light appearing in space. Its position is governed by extending the arm at 45° to the horizontal. The 'A' should be experienced as located where the closed fist of that arm is felt to be – and of the same size as the fist.

With the eyelids partially open, look upward slightly, focusing on the point where the fist would be. The arm is held up until the visualisation becomes reasonably stable. Find the presence of awareness in the appearance of the 'A'.

Two: *the practice of voice*

Sitting in a posture of comfort and alertness – leave the eyes open. Several deep breaths are taken and—having filled the lungs—sing the sound 'A' (*pronounced 'ah'*) and extend that sound to the limit of the breath. Sing the 'A' at a good deep pitch – but not so deep that the voice weakens and breaks up. Find the most comfortable pitch and settle into it. Allow the 'A' to attenuate gradually and disappear into silence. Repeat the 'A' with each out breath. Allow the sense of being to be flooded by the sound of the 'A'. Find the presence of awareness in the dimension of the sound. Whenever distracted – return to the presence of awareness in the dimension of sound. Practise this for five-minute intervals within whatever length sitting session you find comfortable. Enter into the practice of singing the 'A' whenever you become distracted.

Three : the practice of body [19]

Squatting on tiptoe—with the balls of the feet touching and heels touching—balance by touching the ground with the fingertips.

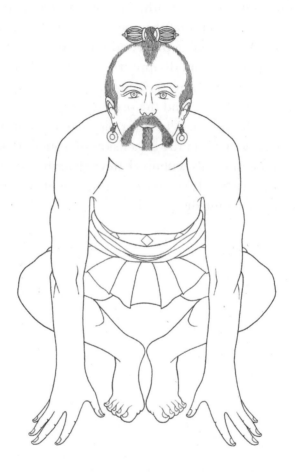

_____

19 This exercise can have fatal consequences. Do not attempt this exercise: if you have a heart condition or high blood pressure; if you are pregnant or menstruating; if you are in any doubt about your physical condition.

When balanced: place the hands palms-down on the knees; straighten the arms; push the knees downward; spread the knees apart. Straightening the back – lean backwards slightly in order to avoid falling forwards.

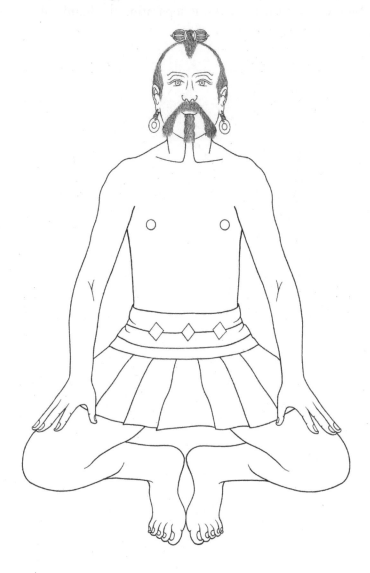

When balanced, the hands are raised above the head. The palms of the hands are placed firmly together about an inch above the head. Ensuring that the fingers are pointing directly upward, attempt, simultaneously, to push the hands upward and the elbows backward – without separating the hands or allowing the hands to rise.

These two movements are matched in effort in order to counteract each other. If equal effort is expended in both attempted movements, the hands and arms will remain in the same position.

Make sure that the fingers point upward whilst increasing the effort – and the hands and arms will begin to judder. The body is then raised until the legs form the same angle as the arms. Remain in this posture until physical collapse occurs. Unless people are experienced trül'khor[20] exponents, this should not take longer than a minute.

Fall back onto a cushion and sit – still stressing the arms. Remain in that posture until it can no longer be held – then fall back into the supine posture: flat on the floor with the arms in whatever position they come to rest. Remain in that posture until breathing and heart rate have returned to normal.

Whilst lying down – simply practise lhatong. Having resumed the sitting posture, simply continue practising lhatong. This practice of *body* is called the vajra or thunderbolt posture.[21] The shape of the posture mirrors the shape of the vajra. It symbolises the indestructibility of the primordial state of awareness. The three spheres of being are often called 'the three vajras', illustrating that the integrated condition of these three spheres of being are beyond conditioning.

The principle of this practice is *nalma*.[22]

---

20 Trül'khor (*'phrul 'khor rNal 'byor, Skt. yantra yoga*) a practice which is similar in some respects to hatha yoga.

21 It takes its name from the vajra – dorje (*rDo rJe*), that accompanies the bell (*drilbu/ dril bu*) in tantric rites. rDo-rJe means literally 'lord stone'.

22 Nalma (*rNal ma*) – the natural state; or zèd pa (*bZad pa*) – the exhaustion of concept.

Through a highly specific method of *exhaustion*, neurotic involvement is weakened with respect to *thought as the definition of being*. In the state of nalma it is difficult to conceptualise. Through nalma therefore, it can become easier to enter into a condition where frames of reference can dissipate. In the state of nalma there is far less interest in generating thought merely to identify and fix reference points.

There is a problem however—in relation to exhaustion—inasmuch as exhaustion tends to cause tiredness. The longer it takes to become exhausted, the longer it takes to recover from exhaustion. The longer it takes to recover, the sleepier one becomes in the process of recovery. Vajra posture solves this problem, inasmuch as it enables us to reach the state of nalma extraordinarily quickly. Because of the speed with which nalma is reached, recovery from symptoms of exhaustion is also surprisingly swift. Because of this we are left feeling energised, clear, and refreshed.

The rapid quality of this practice is crucial – so, if it takes too long to reach the state of nalma, one would need to improve the posture in order that it became more *painful*.

To experience pain is not appealing, but the idea of arriving at the most painful possible position is that as soon as it is found – one collapses. This should occur within seconds rather than minutes. This practice should not cause pain beyond the duration of the exercise – and neither should it cause physical damage. Appropriate pain, in this context, is the pain which athletes experience. Athletic pain, communicates the fact that one is alive in a physical body.

Dzogchen practice is not oriented towards overriding physicality in favour of energy or emptiness. If one does not stress the arms sufficiently, or work to find the exact position which causes most stress to the legs – one would merely hold the posture too long. The principle is to spend as little time as possible in the posture, so that the recovery rate is proportionately fast.

Depending on individual characteristics, different problems will be found with the posture. Those who are stiff and unused to using their bodies may have to squat down with feet slightly apart – rather than adopting the tiptoe position. Those who are simply unfit may have no problem as long as they are fairly supple – and have a sense of balance. Physical balance and emotional balance are interrelated, so it is helpful to practise this exercise daily.

The vajra posture is part of the trül'khor naljor [23] system. This system has some superficial similarities to hatha yoga but it is different in a number of essential respects – especially with regard to vajra posture. Unlike hatha yoga, attainment of the perfect posture is *not* the principle; nalma is the principle. Reaching the state of nalma quickly is one's primary concern. Those who have experience of hatha yoga should not approach vajra posture with the attitude encouraged in that system vis-à-vis the perfect posture.

The principle is *nalma,* so it is important to discover the exact point where the angle of your legs will lead to almost instant collapse.

---

23 Trül'khor naljor (*'phrul 'khor rNal 'byor, Skt. yantra yoga*). Usually found within the anuyoga of the Nyingma Tradition and naljor la'mèd gyüd (*rNal 'byor bLa 'med rGyud,* Skt. anuttrayoga tantras) of the Sarma Schools. The trül'khor method of vajra posture described here is taken from Dzogchen sem-dé.

Those inured to the demands of hatha yoga may be superbly supple – and therefore need to be more exact in the posture. The suppler one is, the more one has to exert oneself in order that the posture *functions*. For the posture to function correctly, awareness is necessary. The posture can be made more acute by perfecting the symmetry. This is achieved by placing the soles of the feet flat together in the same manner as the hands are pressed together – and, by pushing the knees farther apart.

The internal aspect to this practice involves visualising oneself in the form of a dark blue vajra surrounded by sky blue flames. Within the sphere at the centre of the vajra is the sky blue syllable 'Hung'.

On the inhalation the 'Hung' contracts to the size of a fingernail. On exhalation the 'Hung' expands until it becomes larger than the body. One then finds presence of awareness in the visualisation – as inseparable from the sensation of the posture.

Nyi'mèd

Simultaneous awareness [24] of *the clear lake* and *the leaping fish* is the first glimpse of nondual experience. This is the discovery of nyi'mèd – and the vivid portal of Dzogchen.

We should now recapitulate. In our previous discussions of shi-nè and lhatong, we described the manner in which namthogs arise: the fish leaping into existence from emptiness and exploding the surface of the lake. There are immediately three vital considerations: *the still lake*; *the leaping fish*; and, *the awareness which is present in both*.

Before we discuss *the awareness which is simultaneously present in the still lake and the leaping fish*, we should understand something of the context in which these considerations are both actual and illusory. When we say that there are *three* vital considerations, we are speaking from the perspective of the path, rather than from the fruit or result – and in so doing, we are dividing an experience which is actually indivisible. This has to be explained before we can proceed in the attempt to understand nyi'mèd – even though it may appear convoluted to divide a unitary experience purely in order to comprehend its unitary nature.

---

24 Nga chyi'mèd (*sNga phyi 'med*) simultaneity.

As we come closer to the actual practice of Dzogchen, paradox becomes, increasingly, the default medium of communication. The division between *the clear lake* and *the leaping fish* is made in order to define methods of practice.

Due to the fact that practitioners unavoidably approach Dzogchen practice from the perspective of dualism, the experience in which *the still lake and the leaping fish* are indivisible must—of necessity—be presented as two separate experiences. This approach both defines and clarifies the fact that *the clear lake* and *the leaping fish* are not essentially divided.

The fact that *the clear lake* and *the leaping fish* are experienced separately—in order, later, to discern the absence of their division—both defines the dualistic condition [25] of the practitioner and provides the methodology for realising nonduality.

The natural development of lhatong takes us into the phase of experience known as *nyi'mèd*. Nyi'mèd means indivisibility.[26] It is with the practice of nyi'mèd that we approach nonduality and the threshold of the practice of Dzogchen.

With nyi'mèd, what is sought is the lack of difference: between *the quality of the experience of emptiness* and *the quality of the experiences of form*; between *space* and *energy*; between *absence of namthogs* and *movement of namthogs*; and, between *mi-togpa* and *togpa*.

These experiences need to be discovered as having *one taste*.[27] One needs to find oneself in the condition in which one is not distracted from *presence of awareness* – either by mental events or by their absence.

---

25 Nyi-su ma-wa (*gNyis su sMra ba*) dualism or dualistic condition.
26 Nyi'mèd (*gNyis 'med*) – undivided. Nyi means 'two' and 'med means 'not'.
27 Ro gÇig (*ro gCig*).

Even though nyi'mèd is termed a practice – it is not possible to practise nyi'mèd. Nyi'mèd is simply what manifests at a certain stage of practice – and the practice is to recognise that manifest experience. Nyi'mèd occurs when one finds oneself in transition—without design—between nè-pa, the fruitional phase of shi-nè, and gYo-wa, the fruitional phase of lhatong.

This is a natural movement[28] which simply presents itself—of itself—as soon as one finds the presence of awareness in the dimension of the alternation of the sem nyams – the fruitional phases of shi-nè and lhatong.

These fruitional phases are termed: nè-pa[29] (*absence with presence, absence of thought, or presence of awareness*)[30] and gYo-wa, the free non-referential movement of *that which arises in mind.*

Even though nè-pa and gYo-wa are described as fruitional phases, they remain artificial from the perspective of Dzogchen. They are artificial because they are partial experiences. It is only when both are free to alternate—beyond the remit of referentiality—that the uncontrived nature of reality can be said to be present. Having discovered the awareness that is non-separate in the presence of that uncontrived nature, one experiences the one taste of emptiness and form – and they become the *ornaments of rigpa.*[31]

Experiencing emptiness and form as the ornaments of rigpa is by no means easily accessible – and one may therefore, need to experience the alternation of nè-pa and gYo-wa for a considerable duration before such moments of realisation begin to flicker.

---

28 Natural movement – thamal rang 'grö (*tha mal rang 'gros*).
29 Nè-pa (*gNas pa*).
30 See chapter 3.
31 Rig gyan (*rig rGyan*).

65

The one taste of nè-pa and gYo-wa cannot be sought. One cannot actually practise nyi'mèd. One can however, be open to the possibility of experiencing the one taste – and *that* in itself can be described as nyi'mèd. From this perspective, nyi'mèd is simply the capacity to dwell in either mi-togpa or gYo-wa.

Lhundrüp

Lhundrüp is the fourth and final phase of the four naljors.

This phase of practice is the actual practice of Dzogchen. It concerns the integration—of whatever arises in every moment —with the nondual state. Lhundrüp is no longer necessarily a seated posture – but rather the continuity of nyi'mèd into physical activity or into 'ordinary life'.

When lhundrüp becomes feasible – or rather, before it becomes feasible, one finds oneself at the brink of transmission.

To practise lhundrüp one has—in some sense—to leave the framework of the four naljors and seek transmission into the four ting-ngé 'dzin.

5

dzogchen: direct introduction

The four naljors are the practices which are the *principal means of entry* into the practice of Dzogchen sem-dé [1] – the *series of 'the nature of Mind'*. The four ting-ngé 'dzin [2]—the actual practice of Dzogchen sem-dé—comprise nè-pa, [3] mi gYo-wa, [4] nyam-nyid, [5] and lhundrüp. [6]

In the discussion which follows we will leave the approach we took in previous chapters – and present our material as a series of vignettes. Each vignette is a descriptive passage bearing its own heading. Each vignette develops the theme of how the ting-ngé 'dzin could be approached. There is no fixed order in which these vignettes should be read – so the sequence given here can either be followed as it is, or browsed intuitively.

---

1 Dzogchen sem-dé (*rDzogs chen sems sDe*).

2 This exposition of the Aro ting-ngé 'dzin (*A ro ting nge 'dzin*) derives from the Aro ting-ngé 'dzin zhi (*A ro ting nge 'dzin gZhi*), also known as the Aro ying kadag zang thal gyi ting-ngé 'dzin (*A ro dbYings ka dag zang thal gyi ting nge 'dzin*) – Aro absorptions into the dimension of primal purity.

3 Nè-pa (*gNas pa*). Also known as mi-mig-pa'i ting-ngé 'dzin (*mi dMigs pa'i ting nge 'dzin*) – non-conceptual samadhi.

4 Mi gYo-wa (*mi gYo ba*) – unmoving.

5 Nyam-nyid (*mNyam nyid*) – sameness. Also known as zagmèd ting-ngé 'dzin (*zag pa 'med pa'i ting nge 'dzin*) – unconditioned absorption.

6 Lhun grub. Also known as lhundrüp rig-tsal gyi ting-ngé 'dzin (*lhun grub rig rTsal gyi ting nge 'dzin*), absorption of spontaneously present expressions of awareness.

Defining terms

There is no direct word-for-word translation of ting-ngé 'dzin.
It is not a simple term to translate. Ting-ngé 'dzin is the
Tibetan term which equates to 'samadhi' in Sanskrit.
Ting-ngé 'dzin is usually translated as 'absorption' – so we will
begin by examining this word in order to see whether we can
develop *the sense of meaningfulness* required.

There are four meanings of the word 'absorption' in common
usage – and these meanings equate closely with the meaning of
ting-ngé 'dzin. We will therefore take these definitions as
starting points from which we will extrapolate.

Firstly, with regard to the dictionary definition, absorption
carries the sense in which something dry and porous has the
capacity to 'draw moisture into itself'.

Secondly, there is the sense of 'receiving the energy' of an
impact.

Thirdly, there is the state of 'being engrossed'.

Fourthly, there is 'assimilation'.

Strangely enough, these definitions are reflective at some level
of what is implied by the four ting-ngé 'dzin.

The first definition

The first definition relates with emptiness – or nè-pa. This is
the sense in which something dry and porous can absorb
moisture. A sponge has an empty quality. It does not have to be
manufactured or adjusted before it will absorb water.
Absorptiveness is its *natural state*. When it is soaked to capacity
with water, it is essentially no different from its prior state – it
simply holds water within itself.

The second definition

The second definition relates with 'form' – or mi gYo-wa. This is the sense in which something receives the energy of an impact. The power of what arises is freely accommodated. It is already *there*, exactly where it is. Its energy is its movement and the impact is the vividness of its essential condition.

The third definition

The third definition relates with the nondual state of emptiness and form – or nyam-nyid. This is the state in which one is engrossed. This relates to the condition in which subject and object merge – the distinction of observer and observed have dissolved into each other.

The fourth definition

The fourth definition relates with entering into activity – or lhundrüp. Here every aspect of experience is assimilated *of-itself—into itself—by itself*. Everything is assimilated into the condition of rigpa.

Relating the naljors to the ting-ngé 'dzin

If we look carefully at these four phases of ting-ngé 'dzin, they will appear similar to the four naljors. The two series of practices are intimately related, in the sense of running parallel with each other. In order to understand the difference between the naljors and the ting-ngé 'dzin, we need first to explore the ting-ngé 'dzin in terms of how they can be described as the 'results' or the 'fruition'[7] of the naljors. In this sense we could make the following statements: Nè-pa is the fruition of shi-nè. Mi gYo-wa is the fruitional phase of lhatong.

---

7 Drè-bu (*'bras bu*).

gYo-wa and mi gYo-wa

It is important here to clarify the use of the terms gYo-wa and mi gYo-wa in terms of how they are employed respectively within the four naljors and the four ting-ngé 'dzin. When we speak of the four naljors – the initial phase is termed shi-nè and the second lhatong.

The practice of shi-nè leads eventually to the nyam of nè-pa. Once the nyam of nè-pa is experienced and stabilised – the practice of lhatong commences. The practice of lhatong leads eventually to the nyam of gYo-wa.

gYo-wa means movement – and the meaning of this term relates to finding the presence of awareness within the dimension of the movement of *that which arises in mind*.

When we speak of the four ting-ngé 'dzin – the initial phase is termed nè-pa and the second mi gYo-wa.

With respect to the first ting-ngé 'dzin being designated as nè-pa (*the nyam of shi-nè*) one would expect the second ting-ngé 'dzin to be designated as gYo-wa (*the nyam of lhatong*) – but this is not the case.

The second ting-ngé 'dzin is mi gYo-wa – which means not moving. The reason for this is that the terminology of the four naljors is based on the path whilst the terminology of the four ting-ngé 'dzin is fruitional.

From the fruitional perspective gYo-wa and mi gYo-wa are identical in terms of experience. The only difference between gYo-wa and mi gYo-wa is that gYo-wa is *an experience viewed from the perspective of the path* and mi gYo-wa is *the same experience from the perspective of fruition*.

So, gYo-wa is the phase in which total identification with movement occurs as a result of lhatong – and mi gYo-wa is immediate.

Mi gYo-wa could therefore be described as being *unmoved within the movement*.

Nyam-nyid is the fruition of nyi'mèd – because nyam-nyid is immediate. It is not arrived at through lhatong.

Lhundrüp is *in-itself* the fruition of lhundrüp – inasmuch as lhundrüp is immediate and solely fruitional. It can be described as continuous fruition. It is *fruition in-and-of-itself* – and is therefore described *the self-fruition of lhundrüp.*[8]

Nè-pa means 'absence with presence', and equates with being *undisturbed*.

Mi gYo-wa means *unmoving*, and equates with *not being altered by 'that which moves'*.

Nyam-nyid means *nature of the nyams* and equates to *undividedness.*[9]

Lhundrüp means *spontaneity*, and equates with *uninhibited, unimpeded activity.*

Path and fruit

That nè-pa is the fruit of shi-nè, causes a problem in terms of the manner in which nè-pa can be regarded as a practice. The same problem exists in terms of each of the ting-ngé 'dzin, because they are all fruitional.

---

8 Rang drè lhun drüp (*rang 'bras lhun grub*).
9 Undivided with regard to perception and field of perception (*without monistic implication*).

The fruit or result of any practice cannot actually be practised as such, because the end result of anything is theoretically a position of stasis. One can make a journey and arrive at a destination – but having arrived at one's destination, all that can be said is that one 'enjoys being there'.

The journey involves whatever it involves and there is always a sense of time and distance – but with a fruitional path, those aspects of time and space have no direct application. All one can 'do' when one reaches the goal, is to *remain*.[10]

Implicit contradiction

We now come to explore this subject in language which appears ridiculous in ordinary terms, because it systematically contradicts itself. The language we use from this point on will often have to be *felt* rather than intellectually understood.

The logic involved in the following discussions depends entirely upon exactly balanced contradictions which equate precisely with emptiness and form, and the manner in which they cannot be separated.

The practice without practice

The idea of *remaining,* begs questions as to *how* one should *remain* – but no answers are feasible in terms of such questions. Answers are not feasible, simply because answers would not apply. One simply remains through the absence of there being anywhere else to go. This in turn begs questions as to why one should wish to go anywhere else. Here, at least, there are some answers.

---

10 Nal-du zhug (*rNal du gZhugs*), remaining in naturalness. Also ngang né (*ngang gNas*), remaining continuously within the dimension of . . . .

One answer might be that one wishes to depart because one does not regard the point at which one has arrived as the desired destination.

Another answer might be that one feels that one is mistaken in one's understanding of what the destination was said to be.

Yet another answer may be that—having found one's destination—one realises that it is not a desirable destination.

These may well be answers – but they are all ludicrous in the light of practice. So we have answers – but they are answers which lack any useful meaning with regard to the four ting-ngé 'dzin.

That we have arrayed a selection of useless answers is in itself useful, in the sense that we are brought to a point at which we accede to the fact that dualistic reasoning [11] has no function. Whatever we say about the ting-ngé 'dzin will be solely contingent upon meditative experience.[12]

Disorientation

Within the teachings of Sutra and Tantra there is admonishment not to become a 'seeker of nyams'. This advice is given because nyams occur merely as result of practice. If they are actively sought—or if attachment develops toward them—then meditative development halts at that point.

Nyams are unusual experiences. Any practitioner will experience strange or unusual experiential phenomena if they devote sufficient time to practice.

---

11 Nyi-nang (*gNyis sNang*).

12 Ngön sum gyi togpa (*mNgon sum gyis rTogs pa*) – understanding by means of direct perception.

Nyams will also occur under other conditions. They are not limited to meditation, or even to Buddhist meditation.[13] Literally anything which causes disorientation has the potential to give rise to nyams.

Nyams arise via 'disorientation' in terms of habitual tendencies. As soon as referential perceptual mechanisms are released—to whatever degree—the psychophysical fields of the senses begin to *relax*[14] *into their own condition.*

When this *movement* begins, unusual phenomena begin to perform within the sense fields: visual, auditory, olfactory, gustatory, tactile, and conceptual *hallucinations*[15] manifest.

These *hallucinations* can be pleasant, unpleasant, or merely strange.[16] In addition there exist what are termed *spiritual* nyams.[17] These types of nyams are regarded as particularly problematic inasmuch as they can be mistaken for realisation. There are many categories of nyams – and it is not our purpose here to detail them beyond giving a background from which to understand what is meant by the *sem-nyams*.

---

13 It is likely that all religions, if approached with serious intent, incite nyams.

14 Lö-tangwa (*kLod bTang ba*).

15 Gyu ma'i pe (*sGyu ma'i dPe*).

16 Pleasant, unpleasant, or merely strange relate to the three dualistic tendencies: attraction, aversion, and indifference.

17 Ga' nyam su myongpa (*dGa' nyams su Myong pa*) – nyams of bliss; and, nyam kyi nangpa (*nyams kyi sNang pa*) – nyams of ephemeral meditative experience.

The *nyams* of 'the nature of Mind'

The *sem-nyams*[18] comprise two meditative experiences [19] –
emptiness and the non-referential movement of *that which arises
in Mind*. These two meditative experiences need to be
distinguished by the practitioner. Once distinguished – they
need to be understood in terms of moving between them. This
movement occurs naturally – and there is nothing to be done
apart from finding the presence of awareness in whichever
experience is present.

This *natural movement* and finding *the presence of awareness in
whichever experience is present* is the precursor to the realisation
that they are *twin aspects of a prior state*. The prior state is the
state of nonduality – and it is through the realisation of
nonduality that these experiences are experientially redefined.

The nature of this *spontaneous redefinition* shall be clarified at a
further point in this chapter.

The sem-nyams are nè-pa and gYo-wa.

Nè-pa is the nyam of emptiness. gYo-wa is the nyam of form.
Nè-pa is the fruition of shi-nè. gYo-wa is the fruition of
lhatong.

These two experiences are described as *nyams* because they do
not equate with the enlightened state. A nyam, as we have
previously stated, is a meditational experience, meditational
manifestation, or sign of practice.[20]

---

18 Sem nyid-kyi nyams (*sems nyid kyi nyams*) – nyams of the *nature of Mind*. This
terminology is specific to Dzogchen sem-dé as it is presented according to the Aro
gTér.
19 Gom nyams (*sGom nyams*).
20 Drub pa'i tag (*grub pa'i rTags*).

In what way therefore, are we to understand the use of the term *nyam* in relation to nè-pa and gYo-wa? When we discuss the experiences of nè-pa and gYo-wa it can appear as if we are describing states in which referentiality does not occur – yet these states are described as nyams.

What is there then, that prevents nè-pa and gYo-wa being described as rigpa – the nondual state?

When Sutra is discussed, emptiness equates with realisation – so how is it here that nè-pa is not synonymous with rigpa?

We should say immediately, that it is not that emptiness is *not* synonymous with realisation – it is simply that emptiness requires closer definition with regard to the arising of form, and the nature of *that* experience.

When we discuss lhatong, it would seem that we have a state in which the division between observer and observed has dissolved.

So how is it—within this state of referenceless perception of form—that gYo-wa is not synonymous with rigpa?

We should say immediately that it is not that non-referential identification with arising form is *not* synonymous with realisation. It is simply that such identification requires closer definition, with regard to the dissolution of form into emptiness – and the nature of *that* experience.

We have two experiences here which could possibly be rigpa – but in each case the definition rests on the nature of the experience in which they *become each other*. The practice of nyi-mèd simply occurs *of-itself* as the transitional flux of nè-pa and gYo-wa –and within *that* we find ourselves on the brink of discovering their one taste.[21]

---

21 Ro gÇig (*ro gCig*).

The one taste of the two flavours

There are two questions which ask themselves through our practice.

The first question

If we find ourselves in the state of nè-pa and—within that state— namthogs arise – and, if the arising of namthogs immediately becomes the nyam of gYo-wa . . . is this rigpa?

The second question

If we find ourselves in the state of gYo-wa and—within that state— whatever namthogs are present dissolve into emptiness – and, if that empty state immediately becomes the nyam of nè-pa . . . is this rigpa?

The answer to both questions is identical. If one feels that there is *some kind of difference*—and that these states do not constitute a *seamless continuum*—then this is not rigpa.

Rigpa can only be the state in which the difference between nè-pa and gYo-wa vanishes. As soon as the sense of difference between nè-pa and gYo-wa vanishes, one immediately has knowledge of the state, in which nè-pa and gYo-wa are described as *the ornaments of rigpa*.

So when we ask whether emptiness is the realised state – the answer will depend on what occurs when namthogs arise. When we ask whether gYo-wa is the realised state – the answer will depend on what occurs when namthogs dissolve.

The practice of the sem-nyams then, is this: one moves
between the nyams of nè-pa and gYo-wa. This happens *of-itself.*
All one needs to do is to *experientially distinguish*, without
discursively distinguishing—*that*— which is the same within the
two nyams. *That which is the same* is rigpa – instantaneous
presence. Once rigpa is experienced, recognition of the two
nyams as the ornaments of rigpa is simultaneously present.

Hitting the Essence in Three Words

In order to understand the way in which the four ting-ngé 'dzin
are being presented here, we need to explore the *Tsig-sum Né-
dek – Hitting the Essence in Three Words.*[22] This is the
quintessential instruction on Dzogchen left as the final
testimony of Garab Dorje.[23]

Tsig, as in *Tsig-sum Né-dek*, is linguistically unknown in English.
It means a form of expression between *word* and *phrase*. It
refers—in this case—to an extremely concise statement
concerning the meaning of Dzogchen.

The three *words* are these:
> Direct introduction (*to the nondual state*).[24]
> Remaining without doubt (*in the nondual state*).[25]
> Continuing in the state (*of nonduality*).[26]

---

22 Tsig-sum Né-dek (*Tshig gSum gNad du brDeg pa*). This is one of the most widely
known texts concerning direct introduction – ngo-trö (*ngo-sprod*), to Dzogchen, an
extremely concise instruction on self-liberation – rangdröl (*rang grol*).
23 Garab Dorje (*dGa' rab rDo rJe, Skt. Prahevajra*) was the first human teacher of
Dzogchen, and the Buddha of that vehicle of teachings and practices. The *Tsig-sum
Né-dek* was given to his disciple Jampal Shényen (*jam dPal bShes gNyen*, Skt.
Manjushrimitra). Having attained the body of light – öd lü (*'od lus*), Garab Dorje
appeared in the dimension of the sky in front of Jampal Shényen and gave him a
golden casket containing the Tsig-sum Né-dek.
24 Ngo rang thog tu trèd (*ngo rang thog tu sPrad*).
25 Thag gÇig thog tu çèd (*thag gCig thog tu bCad*).
26 Deng dröl thog tu (*gDeng grol thog tu*).

These words represent the base, path, and fruit of Dzogchen. They also relate to the three series of Dzogchen.[27]

Sem-dé emphasises the initial introduction through a variety of methods – non-symbolic, symbolic, and through explanation. The Lama communicates the experience of rigpa to the disciple simply through dwelling in rigpa. Having been introduced to the view in this way, long-dé allows the disciple to experience this awareness through methods which emphasise *sensation*. Through these methods one comes to *remain without doubt* as to the nature of rigpa.

Having actualised the meaning of the view in this way, men-ngak-dé provides the necessary methods to *return to this awareness*; and, having returned to it, to *continue*. In this way, the 'three words' contain the spectrum of Dzogchen teaching in its most concise formulation.

Finding the presence of awareness

The *Tsig-sum Né-dek* is not 'an expression of spirituality' – not as that word is usually understood. It shares a greater commonality with the Northern Lights; with the sound of falling snow; or, with the way in which the sun dazzles the sea.

It is a natural phenomenon. It is reflected in every nuance of our experience. It is so close to us that it is difficult to see.

The instruction in the teaching of trèk chod[28] is given in terms of *finding presence of awareness in the dimension of* . . . a sense field . . . or whatever experiential focus is chosen.

---

27 Direct introduction relates to Dzogchen sem-dé – the base. Remaining without doubt relates to Dzogchen long-dé (*kLong sDe*) – the path. Continuing in the state relates to Dzogchen men-ngak-dé (*man ngag sDe*) – the fruit.
28 Trèk chod (*khregs chod*), cutting the bounds; or, kadag trèk chod (*ka dag khregs chod*), cutting the bounds that inhibit primal purity.

It will be necessary to look at this italicised phrase word-by-word in order to understand what it means.

Finding

Finding is always immediate. If it is not immediate it is called searching or seeking. We can only find what is actually there. If what we seek is there we will find it. In order to explain what this means in this context, we will pose questions and answer them. This will demonstrate something almost banal in its simplicity:

> *Question: "That which I have lost — where is it that I find it?"*
>
> *Answer: "I find it where it is."*
>
> *Question: "Where is it?"*
>
> *Answer: "Where it has always been — or where it has been since you lost track of it."*
>
> *Question: "How do I seek it?"*
>
> *Answer: "Only by knowing where it is."*
>
> *Question: "Now I see it! But where is my sense of not knowing where it was? I cannot remember not knowing where it was."*
>
> *Answer: "Naturally."*
>
> *Question: "Why — how can that be?"*
>
> *Answer: "Because as soon as you found it, you knew it had always been there."*
>
> *Question: "Now I know this — how can I ensure I never forget?"*
>
> *Answer: "Simply forget knowing how not to remember."*

The sequence is similar, whether we speak of rigpa or a concept, a situation, or an object. It could be a word: '*It's on the tip of my tongue . . . I know that I know but I can't find the word. But when I find the word I know it immediately and there is no doubt – I continue in the state of knowing.*' In some ways the discussion of rigpa and the *Tsig-sum Né-dek* is highly mysterious. In another it is so utterly ordinary as to be directly at our fingertips.

Presence

The next word is *presence* – we *find presence*. The word presence refers to being present in all the sense fields. Discovering the nondual state is not a process of internalisation. We do not cut off from the external world. Everything we see, hear, smell, taste, touch, or ideate is undivided from the nondual state – so, to be present, is to be entirely open and embodied.

Awareness

The next word is *awareness* – we *find presence of awareness*. Awareness is the non-discursive, non-referential dwelling in which subject and object / observer and observed are not separate.

Dimension

The next word is *dimension* – we *find presence of awareness in the dimension of . . . .*

The word dimension means totality.[29] Wherever we find presence of awareness becomes the totality. Because wherever we find presence of awareness is totality – it is not possible to be distracted by what lies outside the dimension.

---

29 Dimension – ying (*dByings,* Skt., dhatu).

It is not possible to be distracted by what lies outside the dimension – because the dimension is totality and totality includes everything. If we feel distracted we are not within the dimension – because nothing exists outside the dimension.

Finding presence of awareness in the dimension

There is no way in which this mere indication can be applied. The mere indication is either understood or not. If it is not understood then asking questions would not help. The mere indication is heard—preferably from the Lama in person—and then one enters into practice and finds oneself within the milieu of the mere indication. This is trèk chod.

Emptiness and spaciousness

If we are to understand anything about the self-liberation of *that which arises in Mind*, we must understand something about the experience of awareness itself. In terms of the introduction to rigpa, Dzogchen distinguishes between the conceptual mind (*sems*) and *the nature of Mind (sems nyid)*. One must understand that sems and sems-nyid *also* have one taste.

It is not that self-liberation reduces all phenomena to emptiness.

It is not that *thought* is liberated *of-itself* – and that thereafter it ceases to exist.

It is not that conceptualisation cannot be an ornament of rigpa. If one maintains that conceptual thought is not the efflorescence of the realised state – then one states that duality is not an illusion.

It is not that *sems* is other than *sems nyid*. *Sems nyid* contains *sems*, just as the ocean manifests waves. There is only a problem if one takes *sems* as the totality.

If one takes *sems* to be totality – then one lives within the confines of ever-shifting definitions. These definitions can then be manipulated as interminable attempts to validate being in terms of fixed form.

The spatial dimension should never be understood as emptiness without form.

The words *emptiness* and *spaciousness* are not synonymous with regard to the teaching of Dzogchen.

Spaciousness—and allowing namthogs to dissolve into the spatial dimension—must be understood in terms of nonduality. That is, what 'spaciousness' or 'the spatial dimension' is vis-à-vis nonduality.

When thoughts are self-liberated, they simply become nondual thought – namthogs which are not divided from the *empty origin of namthogs*.

Ocean and waves – sky and clouds

The Dzogchen teachings use two major analogies with regard to mind and *the nature of Mind*: 'waves and the ocean in which they move' and 'sky and the clouds which emerge and dissolve there'.

If we look at Mind as being an ocean, we could say:

> "*Ocean can never be defined by the waves which roll endlessly as its surface. One could study waves into eternity and come no closer to a definition of ocean. All one can say is that waves occur in the ocean and that they are limitless in their forms.*

> "*As soon as we relinquish our attempts to define ocean according to its waves – we realise that waves and ocean are indivisible. Ocean requires no definition – yet waves continually ornament the ocean with their temporary definitions.*"

If we look at Mind as being a sky, we could say:

> "*The sky is vast and beyond limits. Within the unfettered space of the sky there is endless movement. Clouds appear and disappear. They appear from out of the sky and they evaporate back into the sky. The sky is not affected by the clouds which manifest within it – even when it is completely overcast and it appears as if its expansive blueness no longer exists.*
>
> "*Whether we see the sky or not – it remains there, unaltered by that which appears to occlude it. We could take the blue sky to be the perfect state, and yet to be without clouds is not the nature of the sky.*"

Direct introduction

This book cannot be considered to be 'direct introduction'.

This chapter—although entitled 'direct introduction'—is merely a piece of writing *about* direct introduction. It is not direct – and whether it serves to introduce anything, remains merely a possibility.

The same should be said of this paragraph. All that is hoped—at this final point—is to give an impression of how direct introduction might appear, if viewed as a semantic interchange between Lama and disciple.

With the four naljors there is a great deal to explain – but, with the ting-ngé 'dzin, explanation becomes redundant. One needs to have experienced the fruit of shi-nè and lhatong in order to make anything of direct introduction. Without these experiences, introduction by means of the ting-ngé 'dzin is impossible.

A narrative of transmission

A disciple with experience of the four naljors seeks
'pointing-out instructions' [30] – the teaching of the four
ting-ngé 'dzin. This teaching can only be given in the form of
direct transmission.

Having received the direct transmission, the disciple remains
without doubt. If there is doubt, then direct transmission has
not taken place.

If direct transmission has taken place then there will be no
doubt.

Where there is no doubt, all that is left, is to remain – to
continue in the state.

We end this chapter with an allusion to this – but merely an
illusory allusion. The real teaching and real pointing-out
instruction can only be received from one's Lama.

> *The disciple sits before the Lama.*
>
> *The Lama asks a question.*
>
> *The question is simply a word.*
>
> *The word is: "Nè-pa?"*
>
> *There is no answer to this question other than the state of nè-pa.*
>
> *The Lama and disciple enter the state of nè-pa.*
>
> *The Lama asks another question: "Mi gYo-wa?"*
>
> *There is no answer to the question other than the state of mi
> gYo-wa.*
>
> *The Lama and disciple enter the state of mi gYo-wa.*

---

30 Ngo trö nyam (*ngo sProd nyams*).

The Lama asks yet another question: "Now! What is the same?"

Again there is no answer to be given.

The disciple either sees—immediately—what is the same in nè-pa and mi gYo-wa – or not.

The 'answer' for which no spoken word is required is nyam-nyid.

Nyam-nyid is the nature of the sem-nyams which is the nondual state, the state of the Lama and the state of the disciple.

The Lama witnesses the disciple's recognition of nyam-nyid – and says: "Simply remain."

Lhundrüp is spontaneously accomplished.

appendix 1

the historical context of dzogchen sem-dé

The three series of Dzogchen

Dzogchen is divided into three series: sem-dé, long-dé, and men-ngag-dé.[1] These are: the series of the *nature of Mind*, the series of *space*, and the series of *implicit instruction*.

The sem-dé and long-dé series came into Tibet from India in the tenth century – but they have neither been taught widely nor survived as living practice-traditions in the major Nyingma lineages. Both the lineal streams of sem-dé and long-dé declined after the eleventh century, and seem only to have survived in small family lineages.[2]

Dzogchen men-ngag-dé developed later, from the twelfth century, and continued to grow and flourish up to the Tibetan Exodus. Men-ngag-dé is now the pervasive teaching and practice of Dzogchen taught within the major Nyingma lineages.

---

1 Dzogchen sem-dé (*rDzogs chen sems sDe*), Dzogchen long-dé (*rDzogs chen kLong sDe*), and Dzogchen men-ngag-dé (*rDzogs chen man ngag sDe*).
2 All three series of Dzogchen have survived as practice lineages in the Bön Tradition.

Since the Tibetan diaspora men-ngag-dé has also waned in favour of the growing emphasis on mahayoga in the major Nyingma lineages.[3]

Vairotsana[4] was a key figure in the dissemination of Dzogchen sem-dé. He is considered to have brought the sem-dé and long-dé teachings from India to Tibet. During the reign of Chögyal[5] Trisong Détsen in the eighth century, he was ordained by Shantarakshita as one of the first seven monks in Tibet at the newly founded Sam-yé monastery. This does not imply that Vairotsana remained a monk for the rest of his life. It was customary for practitioners at the time of the 'early spread' of the teachings in Tibet to take on monasticism for a limited period, before moving into their tantric phase. This had been the Vajrayana custom of practice in India. Becoming a monk, or a nun as in the case of Yeshé Tsogyel, represented the sutric phase of their training.

---

3 Lopön Ögyen Ten'dzin Rinpoche, a Tibetan Lama of our acquaintance, received the lung (*rLung*, Skt. agama) transmission of scriptural authorisation or reading transmission of the twenty-one sem 'dzin from Düd'jom Rinpoche. (*bDud 'joms jigs bral ye shes rDo rJe*, 1904–1987, *was one of Tibet's foremost yogis, scholars, and meditation masters – and an incarnation of Traktung Düd'jom Lingpa*, 1835–1904.) Sadly, however, Düd'jom Rinpoche passed away before Lopön Ögyen Rinpoche could receive the tri (*sGom khrid – precise and detailed explanation of practice*) from him. He asked many Nyingma Lamas whether they could provide the tri – but found it to be unavailable, as far as he had searched.

4 Vairotsana of Pagor (*sPa gor ba'i ro tsa na*) was a Tibetan translator living during the reign of Trisong Détsen. He was one of the 25 disciples of Padmasambhava and a lineage holder of trül'khor. Vairotsana's chief disciples were Yudra Nyingpo (*gYu sGra sNying po*), Sangtön Yeshé, Jnana Kumara of Nyag (*nyag ye she gZhon nu*), and Lady Yeshe Drönma (*jo mo ye shes sGron ma*). An especially renowned disciple was the octogenarian Pang Mi'pham Gönpo (*sPang mi 'pham mGon po*), whose disciples attained rainbow body for seven generations by means of the oral instructions of the Dzogchen long-dé teaching: Dorje Zampa (*rDo rJe zam* pa) – vajra bridge.

5 Chögyal (*chos rGyal*) – Buddhist King.

Vairotsana was a prolific translator and siddha. Trisong Détsen sent him to India, accompanied by another practitioner, to receive teachings from Shri Simha on Dzogchen sem-dé and long-dé. These teachings were given to them at night with the utmost secrecy.

Shri Simha wrote down the 'Eighteen Esoteric Instructions' of the *series of the nature of Mind* on white silk using milk from a white goat. The words only became clear when held over smoke. This teaching comprises the eighteen texts known as the 'Sem-dé Chö-gyèd'. These are composed of the 'Five Early Translations' translated by Vairotsana, and the 'Thirteen Later Translations'[6] compiled by Dri'mèd Shényèn,[7] the eighth century Dzogchen yogi born in Northwestern India. He had received transmission of Dzogchen from Shri Simha,[8] Jnanasutra,[9] Sangwa Sang-gyé,[10] and Mahasiddha Lilavajra.[11]

---

6 'The Thirteen Later Translations' – chi-gyür chu sum (*phyi 'gyur bCu gSum*) of the 'Eighteen Major Scriptural Transmissions of the Mind Series' – sem dé lung chenpo cho gye (*sems sDe lung chen po bCo brGyad*).

7 Dri'mèd Shényèn (*dri 'med bShes gNyen*, Skt. Vimalamitra) translated, together with Ma Rinchen Chog, important Nyingma texts, such as the 'Sangwa Nyingpo' (*gSang ba sNying po*, Skt. Guhyagarbha), 'Heart Essence of Secrets'.

8 Shri Simha (*shri sing ha*) was a principal disciple of Jampal Shényèn (*'jam dPal bShes gNyen*, Skt. Manjushrimitra) in the Dzogchen lineage. Jampal Shényèn and Shri Simha were already independently active in India. Jampal Shényèn however, was a learned scholar before becoming a disciple of Garab Dorje (*dGa' rab rDo rJe*, Skt. Prahevajra). He came from Oddiyana in Eastern Afghanistan. Shri Simha was born and resided for some time in the Chinese region of Northern India; Jampal Shényèn visited China before and after he came to Tibet and transmitted the Dzogchen teachings at Sam-yé.

9 Yeshé mDo (*ye shes mDo*, Skt. Jnanasutra, 5th to 6th century) was a disciple of Shri Simha and a vajra brother of Dri'mèd Shényèn.

10 Sangwa Sang-gyé (*gSangs ba sang gyé*, Skt. Buddhaguhya).

11 Lilavajra (*sgeg pa'i rDo rJe*) was an eighth century mahasiddha from Oddiyana who wrote commentaries on the Guhyagarbha Tantra.

Dri'mèd Shényèn was invited to Tibet by emissaries of Chögyal Trisong Détsen.[12] Dri'mèd Shényèn became established as a teacher and translator of Dzogchen texts.

The reason for secrecy

There have been many critics of Dzogchen in Tibet, throughout its history, who have held the opinion that Dzogchen is a heresy. This contention continues to the present day in certain quarters. In response to the fervour of critics over a millennium, Nyingma scholars have argued the position of Dzogchen as an authentic Buddhist vehicle employing the language and metaphysical constructs of both Sutra and Tantra. As a result, Dzogchen has become gradually more academic and ritualised from the time of Jig'mèd Lingpa [13] onwards.

The problem for conventionalist religion [14]—and hierarchic institutions of social control—is that Dzogchen teachings transcend the idea of karma as 'inescapable cause and effect'.

---

12 Emperor Trisong Détsen (*khri srong lDe bTsan*), son of Mé Ag Tshom (*mes ag tshom*), ruled from 755 to 804. Mé Ag Tshom (*son of Tridu Songtsen and Queen Chim gZa' Tènma Thog-thog Teng*) gained the appellation Mé Ag Tshom owing to his being outlandishly hirsute. Trisong Détsen—second of the three Dharma monarchs of Tibet—played a vital rôle in establishing the Nyingma Tradition. He had five wives including Yeshé Tsogyel—Princess of Kharchen—who became Padmasambhava's consort and the female tantric Buddha.

13 Jig'mèd Lingpa (*'jigs 'med gLing pa*, 1730–1798) is one of the important figures in the Nyingma Tradition. He was a profound scholar and visionary, who received the Longchen Nyingthig cycle of teachings and practices as gTérma from Longchenpa (*kLong chen rab 'byams pa*, 1308–1364). With the patronage of the Dergé royal family, Jig'mèd Lingpa compiled the Nyingma Gyübum and composed its accompanying catalogue.

14 Jig'ten gyi kun Dzokyi tenpa (*'jig rTen gyi kun rDzob kyi bDen pa*).

The word karma is often misconstrued to mean a moralistic acceptance that *'my situation (and the situation of others) is as it is – and arises solely from past actions'*.

The corollary to this is that, since past actions cannot be changed, one's current situation cannot be changed – and consequently, there is no purpose in endeavouring to change anything. This view of karma can lead to a callous position in which one does not need to feel sympathy – on the grounds that the situation of others is their own fault. Also, this view suits a feudal society in which life runs smoothly when everyone accepts their place.

Obviously, Dzogchen is dangerous from this point of view. Dzogchen states that liberation is possible within one lifetime – and this possibility means that a person can become free of their societal limits as well as their experiential limits. The idea that karma is not a *materialistic system of cause and effect*—but an *experiential correlation of perception and response*—was threatening to the socio-religious hierarchy. If one could escape karma through dissolving the state of mind which gave rise to the karma, then there was no reason why people should accept that their lowly feudal social status was karmic in origin and unchangeable. If it is not karma which fixes one's social status then social reform becomes possible – and this idea would be unwelcome to a feudal elite wishing to maintain the status quo.

The contention—vis-à-vis Dzogchen—that karma was the 'form aspect' of *patterning* in relation to the 'emptiness aspect' of *chaos*, was not judged to be conducive to maintaining social order. Dzogchen transmission therefore had to be given in secret – as it was deemed too dangerous for the general population.

It would seem to be a perennial policy amongst all socially repressive cultures to keep people ignorant and bound in materialistic superstitions of punishment and retribution.

The actual meaning of karma is *habituated perception and response* [15] – which is to say: how we interpret information, objects, situations, or persons dictates how we respond to them. The hypothesis that everything which occurs is the result of previous actions means that realisation would have to be the result of karma. This is antithetical to Buddhism, as realisation would then be dependent upon a dualistic cause. Karma disappears as soon as the *perception-mind-of-karma* disappears.

Owing to the need for secrecy vis-à-vis Dzogchen, Shri Simha gave Vairotsana empowerment and instruction from the tantric vehicle during the day – and from Dzogchen by night. Before returning to Tibet, Vairotsana also met Garab Dorje, the first human teacher of Dzogchen, from whom he received further teachings.

On Vairotsana's return, he taught everything that he had received, also in secrecy, and translated the first Dzogchen sem-dé texts into Tibetan.

Racist ecclesiastics in India saw Dzogchen as 'culturally Indian' and wanted to prevent access to its teachings because they feared that Dzogchen could be lost to their country if it were proliferated in Tibet. This view would mean that they believed Dzogchen was a commodity which could be owned. Dzogchen however, being the primordial state, is owned by everyone – but this is not a concept that settles well in a feudal society.

---

15 This is true not only of Dzogchen – but also of Theravada Buddhism.

To undermine the spread of Dzogchen teaching in Tibet, the reactionary faction spared no effort in having Vairotsana discredited. They spread the rumour that he had merely imported a compilation of black-magic spells. This is understandable in that many people today also hold opinions that have little or no relation to reality – but it is even easier to understand when one considers the fact that most Tibetans, including the aristocracy, were illiterate at the time in question. Had they been literate, they would have recognised the ridiculousness of such assertions.

Chögyal Trisong Détsen's ministers felt that Vairotsana should be executed – but the Chögyal disagreed and contrived to have a beggar—physically resembling Vairotsana—thrown into the river [16] whilst Vairotsana himself hid in a hollow pillar within the palace. One night the Queen discovered him there. She informed the ministers – and the Chögyal was thus forced to agree to Vairotsana's expulsion to Tshawarong in Eastern Tibet.[17] While in exile in Tshawarong, Vairotsana accepted Yudra Nyingpo [18] as a disciple.

Yudra Nyingpo was eventually responsible for helping Vimalamitra translate the later texts of Dzogchen sem-dé into Tibetan, whilst also working towards helping his teacher return from exile.

---

16 An explanation of this behaviour does not seem to be addressed in the texts, in terms either of bodhicitta or skilful means – or wisdom and method.

17 Tibet, like most mediæval societies, was subject to capricious behaviour on the part of those in power – be they Buddhist or otherwise.

18 Yudra Nyingpo (*gYu sGra sNying po*) was a prince of Gyarong in Eastern Tibet and was one of the principal translators of the first translation stage of texts into Tibetan.

At this time, Vairotsana also gave Pang Mi'pham Gönpo [19] oral instruction on the Dzogchen long-dé. Pang Mi'pham Gönpo— the Invincible Geriatric—was a physically frail 85-year-old man when he started to practise, so the meditation belt and a stick which were part of the transmission proved extremely useful. Many people imagine that Vairotsana gave him the meditation belt and a stick to prop up his chin—and hold him in position because of his age—but this is not accurate. The belt and stick are an essential aspect of long-dé practice, and are used by practitioners of all ages. The meditation belt is called a gom-tag and the stick is called a gom-ten (*meditation support*) or gom-shing (*meditation stick*). There are gom-tags of various lengths and also different kinds of gom-ten. These are used in various combinations to facilitate a series of highly specific meditation postures which co-ordinate body posture with the functioning of the rTsa-rLung system (*spatial nerves and spatial winds*).

In 1971, Kyabjé Düd'jom Rinpoche told Ngak'chang Rinpoche: *"Pang Mi'pham Gönpo's family laughed at the idea of his starting to practise at such a late stage in life – but he achieved liberation nonetheless! Pang Mi'pham Gönpo said that at this time he became immensely joyful, and embraced Vairotsana – not letting go for a day. He lived for a further hundred years, transmitting the Dzogchen teachings to his own disciples. Each one of them achieved rainbow body."*

Vairotsana also transmitted the sem-dé teachings to Nyag Yeshé Zhön-nu,[20] who was born in Yarlung in the late eighth century and became a brilliant translator. In his late twenties – he, like Vairotsana, had to spend time in exile after Trisong Détsen died. His life was not easy.

---

19 Pang Mi'pham Gönpo (*sPang mi 'pham mGon po*).
20 Nyag Yeshé Zhön-nu (*gNyag ye shes gZhon nu*).

Nyag Yeshé Zhön-nu's brother took a violent dislike to him and declared that he was 'an adept of extremist mantras'. He regained the confidence of the people by manifesting precious gems where he lived – but his bad luck persisted and he was pursued by antagonists. Fortunately, he met Dri'mèd Shényèn in the course of his travels and received teachings from him.

Nubchen Sang-gyé Yeshé,[21] a student of one of Nyag Yeshé Zhön-nu's disciples, also received teachings from Padmasambhava, Yeshé Tsogyel, and many other masters; eventually he became a prolific writer on Dzogchen sem-dé.

Later, when King Langdarma persecuted the monastic institutions of Tibet, it was through Nubchen Sang-gyé Yeshé's actions that the gö kar chang lo'i dé [22] was unharmed, though his own two sons were killed during the king's reign. Nubchen Sang-gyé Yeshé terrified the king by pointing a finger at the sky and bringing forth a black iron scorpion the size of nine yaks. He also demonstrated how he could manifest a thunderbolt and use it to pulverise rocks. This demonstration was sufficient to deter Langdarma from persecuting the gö kar chang lo'i dé.

Aro Yeshé Jung-né [23] was a teacher and writer on sem-dé in the tenth century. His system of teaching was known as Kham-lug, because he originated from the Kham region of Tibet. He formulated a system of sem-dé known as the Seven Sessions of Aro. His teachings and writings had a profound influence on Dzogchen sem-dé but his life remains obscure.

---

21 Nubchen Sang-gyé Yeshé (*gNubs chen sangs rGyas ye shes*).
22 Gö kar chang lo'i dé (*gos dKar lCang lo'i sDe*), the series or division of long hair and white skirts.
23 Aro Yeshé Jung-né is unrelated to Drüpchen Aro Yeshé – the son and Dharma heir of Aro Lingma, the female gTértön (*gter ston*) – treasure discoverer, who revealed the Aro gTér.

Rong-zom Chökyi Zangpo,[24] a great master of Dzogchen in the eleventh century, was known as an emanation of Jampalyang because from the age of eleven he was able to remember teachings after hearing them only once. He also possessed great siddhis and, during the 119 years that he lived, he had many students, wrote prolifically, and developed the system of teaching known as Rong-lug.

Many more lines of the lineage branched out after this, but after the eleventh century it declined. By the seventeenth century, the sem-dé had become extinct as a separate living tradition.

Ögyen gTérdag Lingpa,[25] one of the great Nyingma gTértöns, stated that practically nothing survived of Dzogchen sem-dé in his day—the seventeenth century—apart from the transmission of the *lung*.[26]

The Chögyals

The period in which Padmasambhava and Yeshé Tsogyel dwelt in Tibet was an unprecedented period of growth in that country – spiritually, culturally, and in terms of prosperity. This trend continued—although to a lessening degree—down to Trisong Détsen's grandson Chögyal Tri Ralpaçan.

---

24 Rong-zom Chökyi Zangpo (*rong zom chos kyi bZang po*, 1012–1088) was born in Tsang Rong and mastered both Nyingma and Sarma traditions. He translated many works on Vajrayana, some of which are preserved in the Kangyur. Sadly, much of his original writing has been lost – but still extant is his commentary on the Guhyagarbha Tantra, his introduction to Mahayana, and his 'Establishing All Appearances as Immaculate' – nang-wa lhar drup (*sNang ba lhar sGrub*).
25 Ögyen gTérdag Lingpa (*O rGyan gTer bDag gLing pa* 1646–1714) was the speech incarnation of Vairotsana. His mother was Yum Lha'dzin Yangchen Drölma, a direct descendent of Trisong Détsen. His father, Sangdag Thrin-lé Lhundrüp, was the incarnation of Nubchen Sang-gyé Yeshé, one of the 25 disciples of Padmasambhava.
26 Lung (*rlung*), permission to practise.

Chögyal Tri Ralpaçan[27] was utterly devoted to preserving and enhancing the Vajrayana heritage of Padmasambhava and Yeshé Tsogyel, and to propagating the 'dülwa'i dé and ngak kyi dé[28] as the two authentic wings of Dharma. The pivotal act which led to Langdarma's decision to have his brother assassinated was Ralpaçan's public display of placing the 'dülwa'i dé and the ngak kyi dé above the Chögyal. Ralpaçan unwound his hair and laid it out along the seats on either side of him. To the ends of his tresses he attached long ribbons in order that the 'dülwa'i dé and the ngak kyi dé could sit on either side of him. This symbolism displayed the 'dülwa'i dé and the ngak kyi dé as being higher in status than the rex divus cælestis (*god descended from the sky*). This display, although threatening to the old order, was nothing new. Padmasambhava had set the precedent on his arrival in Tibet, and Ralpaçan was simply re-enacting his grandfather's abdication from divine right.

When Padmasambhava first arrived in Tibet, everyone offered prostrations – apart from Trisong Détsen. Trisong Détsen had invited Padmasambhava to come to Tibet and was sincerely enthusiastic about his arrival, so his failure to offer prostrations was not exactly an act of arrogance on his part. He had merely failed to comprehend that his rôle as a *god descended from the sky* was utterly irrelevant in terms of the Dharma he wished to practise.

---

27 Chögyal Tri Ralpaçan (*Chos rGyal khri ral pa can*, 815–841), was an embodiment of Chana Dorje (*phyag na rDo rJe*, Skt. Vajrapani) and the third great Dharma King of Tibet. He built new gompas; renewed many old gompas and hermitages; and invited many Indian masters to Tibet.
28 'dülwa'i dé (*'dul ba'i sDe*) – celibate Sutrayana practitioners; ngak kyi dé (*sNgags kyi sDe*) – non-celibate Vajrayana practitioners.

Be that as it may – Padmasambhava helped Trisong Détsen transcend his incomprehension by singeing his beard with a sheet of flame emitted from his fingertips. Trisong Détsen prostrated immediately – and at that point the rôle of rex divus cælestis ended. Trisong Détsen was still the Chögyal of Tibet – but he was no longer the ultimate spiritual authority. He was no longer to be worshipped as if the well-being of Tibet was dependent upon the Chögyal's well-being. Ralpaçan's brother Langdarma is often portrayed as an advocate of Bön – and therefore ostensibly anti-Buddhist. It was however, not Buddhism per se to which Langdarma took objection; it was the fact that Buddhism had superseded the institution of god king. Langdarma was therefore an advocate of divine monarchy (*and the sacristans whose rôle it was to serve the god king*). The idea of religion taking precedence over the god king was anathema to Tibetan culture, and it was only the spiritual power of Padmasambhava and Yeshé Tsogyel which had ever made the social enormity of this reversal possible. In terms of Tibetan culture, religion was there to serve the god king and to ensure his long life for the benefit of the people of Tibet. To invert this—from the point of view of pre-Buddhist culture—was to court disaster for Tibet. This superstition may have had less influence had it not been for the fact that the Tibetan empire was crumbling during the reign of Ralpaçan, and serious inroads were being made into most territories which Tibet had previously annexed.

In respect of the rex divus cælestis, the historical rôle of the pre-Buddhist Tibetan kings was strikingly similar to the pharaohs of Ancient Egypt – but few parallels could be made in terms of their respective societies.

It is not the purpose of this essay to define Bön—either during the Nga-dar[29] or prior to it—or to purvey a limited and misleading understanding of Bön – but one section of the Bön clergy existed solely to serve the god king, acting as intermediaries between the god king and the aristocracy.

That Buddhism presents an extremely unfavourable image of Langdarma is entirely reasonable in terms of his assassination of a great Buddhist king, but it is likely that Langdarma saw himself as a Tibetan patriot rather than an entirely self-serving regicide and scheming pretender to the throne. He may well have desired the throne, but he also desired a strong country which would keep its empire intact. He saw Buddhism as undermining the autonomy and security of the country that his heirs would inherit.

Langdarma saw the monasteries as a vast drain on national resources – which indeed they were. The royal treasury was under great pressure to fund foreign wars – and wars were obviously not of central importance to a religion which advocated peace. From Langdarma's point of view, peace meant not taking action against those territories which were in revolt against Tibetan dominion. It would require significant resources to preserve the Tibetan empire through military strength, and Langdarma saw the taxes deployed to maintain monasteries as squandering resources on the very cause of the country's enfeeblement.

It might not be entirely out of the question to suggest that Langdarma also deemed the taxation required to support monasticism to be an unreasonable burden on the landholders.

---

29 Nga-dar (*sNga dar*) – the First Spread of Buddhism in Tibet.

Also the non-Buddhist landholders doubtless petitioned Langdarma for support in the face of growing taxation. Later histories written by Sarma commentators—who gloss over the First Spread—level accusations against Ralpaçan to the effect that it was his zeal in respect of excessive monastic expansion which led to Langdarma's attack on Buddhism and the consequent collapse of Tibet as a unified nation. Langdarma was therefore primarily interested in the abolition of monastic power and the reinstatement of the god king. Accordingly, it was mainly the monasteries that were suppressed upon Langdarma's succession to the throne – rather than the gö kar chang lo'i dé.

Individual gö kar chang lo practitioners and Lamas such as Nubchen Sang-gyé Yeshé continued in their activities unhindered. They studied, practised, taught, and gave empowerment privately and were not subject to government interference. The gö kar chang lo'i dé were largely self-supporting and did not rely on institutions. They therefore did not concern the god king. Neither did they pose a threat to the god king which would warrant the time and effort involved in hunting them down across Tibet's vast mountainous terrain.

Styles of ordination

Dzogchen sem-dé was brought to Tibet at a time when Buddhism proliferated. It was during this time that the ordained Nyingma sanghas were established.

The ordained practitioners were: the monks and nuns whose ordination was based within the sutras; the ngakpas and ngakmas (*sNgags pa and sNgags ma or sNgags mo*) whose ordination was based within the mahayoga tantras; and the naljorpas and naljormas (*rNal 'byor pa and rNal 'byor ma*) whose ordination was based within the anuyoga tantras. There were, in addition, non-ordained practitioners.

From the point of view of Dzogchen, ordination was not a requirement of practice – since Dzogchen (*being the path of self-liberation*) is not primarily concerned with symbolism. The historical records of this time are not explicit in their descriptions of which type of practitioner the great lineage holders were. Both Vairotsana and Nyag Yeshé Zhön-nu are said to have been ordained as monks. In line drawings however, from Düd'jom Rinpoche's *History and Fundamentals of the Nyingma School of Tibetan Buddhism*,[30] all but Vairotsana are depicted with long hair and yogic dress. It would therefore seem that most of these practitioners by the latter part of their lives belonged either to the gö kar chang lo'i dé or to the non-robed Dzogchen style of practice.

The two Nyingma sanghas are the 'dülwa'i dé and the ngak kyi dé. The 'dulwa'i dé is the 'series or division of vinaya' – the Sutrayana renunciates with shaven heads. The ngak kyi dé is the 'series or division of mantra' – the Vajrayana sangha whose practice is founded on yeshé (*ye shes – primordial wisdom*).

---

30 Wisdom Publications, 1991.

The ngak kyi dé is also known as: the gö kar chang lo'i dé (*gos dKar lCang lo'i sDe*), the series or division of long hair and white skirts; the gendün karpo (*dGe 'dun dKar po*), the white sangha – in contradistinction to the gendün marpo (*dGe 'dun dMar po*), which is the red sangha of monastics; and the ngak'phang gendün (*sNgags 'phang dGe 'dun*), the mantra hurling assembly. Ngak'phang is an archaic term and, now, is not widely understood even within the Nyingma Tradition.

During the Nga-dar, the ngak kyi dé comprised two streams of practice. The ngakpa and ngakma ordination was based in mahayoga, and the naljorpa and naljorma ordination was based in anuyoga. Dzogchen was common to both streams. The Nga-dar extended from the seventh to the eleventh century, and the ngak kyi dé thrived throughout that period despite the brief persecution of Langdarma.

It should be understood that there have been monastic and non-monastic practitioners from the very inception of Dharma. The division of the sangha into 'dülwa'i dé and ngak kyi dé was not unique to Tibet. The 'dülwa'i dé and ngak kyi dé date back directly to Shakyamuni Buddha.

It is not an obscure fact that Shakyamuni Buddha's principal followers were by no means all members of the 'dülwa'i dé. Dri'mèd Drakpa [31] is one example of a preëminent non-celibate practitioner. Dri'mèd Drakpa was not simply a non-celibate practitioner, but a merchant by livelihood – and it was he who defeated the great monastic scholar Shariputra in debate on the subject of emptiness.

---

31 Dri'mèd Drakpa (*Dri 'med grags pa*), Skt. Vimalakirti.

It could be said that Dri'mèd Drakpa was the prototype mahasiddha, for not only was he non-celibate, but he was also a householder and a businessman – thoroughly outwardly immersed in the world of commerce. That his attainment was unimpaired and unimpeded by his so-called worldly involvement is the original and most powerful precedent for the non-monastic sangha. Dri'mèd Drakpa was the author of the highly esteemed Drima 'mèd par Dragpa Tenpa'i mDo.[32]

On various occasions, he challenged the understanding of every major disciple of Shakyamuni Buddha and each was found wanting at some point of understanding. All disciples of Shakyamuni Buddha were in agreement that Dri'mèd Drakpa had the highest understanding of the disciples, and concurred that they had been corrected through his unparalleled nondual wisdom and insight.

Approaching Dzogchen sem-dé

Sem-dé is composed of detailed teachings on the *nature of Mind, sem-nyid,* and how that is differentiated from conceptual mind, *sem.*

It describes how dualistic mind is affected by practice, with regard to the sem-nyams [33] – the *direct experience of emptiness* [34] and the *direct experience of the movement of namthogs* through which one discovers the *instant-presence* of rigpa.

---

32 Drima 'mèd par Dragpa Tenpa'i mDo (*dri ma med par grags pas bsTan pa'i mDo*), Vimalakirti Nirdesha or Vimalakirti's Teaching Sutra.
33 Sems nyams (*abbreviation of sems nyid nyams*).
34 Emptiness – tongpa-nyid (*sTong pa nyid*), Skt. shunyata.

In the Aro gTér, the teachings on sem-dé are divided into two parts. The first of these is the practice of the ngöndro of Dzogchen sem-dé – the preliminary practices which are entitled the four naljors.[35] The second part is the definitive practice of sem-dé – the four ting-ngé 'dzin. The purpose of ngöndro practice in any vehicle is to bring the condition of the practitioner to the base of that vehicle.

The tantric ngöndro, which is the one most widely known in the West, brings practitioners to the base of Tantra, which is the experience of emptiness. It bridges the experiences of the previous vehicle, Sutra, and, because it is the tantric ngöndro, it is tantric in its nature. For example, the practice of Lama'i naljor[36] is tantric – inasmuch as it centres on union with the mind of the Lama, through visualisation and mantra.

Likewise, the four naljors contain detailed teachings on the nature of Mind – which bridge the experiences gained in both Sutra and Tantra. This allows the practitioner to arrive at the base of Dzogchen, which is the nondual experience, and then to begin the actual sem-dé practice of the four ting-ngé 'dzin: *nè-pa, mi gYo-wa, nyam-nyid,* and *lhundrüp.*

In the same way as the tantric ngöndro resembles the practice of Tantra, the Dzogchen ngöndro resembles the practice of Dzogchen. The fourth naljor is lhundrüp, which is the integration of the nondual experience into everyday life. This, of course, is none other than the practice of Dzogchen itself.

Dzogchen teachings consequent to the seventeenth century were mostly Dzogchen men-ngag-dé: the *series of implicit instruction.*

---

35 Aro naljor zhi ngöndro (*A ro rNal 'byor bZhi sNgon 'gro*).
36 Lama'i naljor (*bLa ma'i rNal 'byor*), Skt. guru yoga.

The word 'implicit' is used because the meaning of the instruction is only accessible to the practitioner who is able to perceive it. In other words, it is not hidden but neither is it explicit – it is *implicit*. The transmission of understanding the practices is contained in the instruction of the practice itself.

An example of this is the teaching on the four Çôg-zhag.[37] This is given to the disciple by the teacher in a cryptic manner according to the four Çôg-zhag.[38] These are composed of Mountain Çôg-zhag, Ocean Çôg-zhag, Instantaneous-presence Çôg-zhag, and Vision Çôg-zhag.

Mountain Çôg-zhag is the Çôg-zhag of the body: whatever the position of the body is the perfect posture for integration with rigpa.

Ocean Çôg-zhag is the Çôg-zhag of the eyes: wherever the eyes are directed is the perfect placement of the gaze for integration with rigpa.

Instantaneous-presence Çôg-zhag is the Çôg-zhag of the focus of the eyes: wherever the eyes focus is where their focus is found – whatever the content of Mind is spontaneously integrated with rigpa.

Vision Çôg-zhag is the Çôg-zhag in which body, vision, and Mind are seamlessly integrated with rigpa.

This is a crude example of the teaching of the four Çôg-zhag. The *implicit instruction* is that there is nothing either to change or to alter.

There is nothing to do, nowhere to go, no practice to follow.

---

37 Çôg-zhag (*cog bZhag bZhi*).
38 Direct transmission from a Lama is required for this practice.

If this is not immediately understood, questions are useless – there are no answers beyond direct communication of the four Çôg-zhag. There is nothing to ask because there is nothing to do beyond recognising that you have never been anywhere other than the state of rigpa. If the practitioner is in the nondual state, then of course there is nothing to do, and nowhere else to go.

Dzogchen men-ngag-dé contains no detailed teachings on mind and the nature of Mind; thus it is much harder to access the meaning of the teaching, and to explore and practise in relation to an evolving understanding. In fact, it is impossible to practise men-ngak-dé if one has no experience of the nondual state. Unless one first practises either the sem-dé ngöndro or the vehicles of Sutra and Tantra, one is unlikely to find the nondual state; the nondual state is the springboard necessary to understand and practise the men-ngag-dé teachings.

This goes some way towards explaining why most of the teaching available on Dzogchen at this time is cryptic and introduced within the context of tantric training. It also explains why many Nyingma Lamas are so reluctant to teach Dzogchen. The methods of Dzogchen men-ngak-dé are extremely simple and direct, and could easily be misunderstood. The four Çôg-zhag are a skeletal frame clothed by many sem'dzin (*methods of men-ngag-dé*). These methods are secret – not because they are dangerous, but because the power of transmission would be jeopardised if they were given to people who could not comprehend them.

appendix ii

sNying mDo

the heart essence of
unconventional wisdom

Chenrézigs—absorbed in the contemplation of unconventional wisdom—perceived duality as empty. On seeing this directly, he turned to Shariputra saying: "*Form is emptiness and emptiness is form.*"

Then—in order to clarify—he continued: "*Form is not different from emptiness; emptiness, not different from form. That which appears as emptiness is form – and that which appears as form is emptiness. You will not find emptiness apart from form – nor form apart from emptiness. The psychology of duality, sensation, sense connections, thought, and consciousness – these are also emptiness and form. So Shariputra – you can only characterise form in terms of emptiness – and emptiness in terms of form.*

The phenomena of reality are neither existent nor non-existent. They are neither pure nor impure. They neither increase nor decrease. Psychological attributes are neither existent, nor non-existent. The perceptions of eyes, ears, nose, tongue, body, and mind – are both reality and illusion. Likewise, form, sound, colour, taste, touch, and objects. Likewise, the dimension of vision and awareness.

There is neither understanding, nor absence of understanding. There is no suffering, old age, or death – nor do they end. There is neither merit, nor accumulation of merit. There is no annihilation, no path, and no wisdom. There is neither realisation nor non-realisation. There is neither attainment nor absence of attainment.

Because the liberated Mind-warrior's awareness is characterised by this unconventional wisdom – even the four philosophical extremes are not perceived as dualism. Likewise, all those who realise nonduality—in the past, present, and future—dwell in the knowledge of unconventional wisdom, which is none other than rigpa.

So Shariputra, relax. Relax in the knowledge that unconventional wisdom is the great mantra, the mantra of completion, the mantra of totality, the mantra which expresses everything. Unconventional wisdom dissolves all struggles. It is true, simply because it lacks the complication of falsity. This is the essence of unconventional wisdom."

A: Ga-té, Ga-té, Para Ga-té,

Para-sam Ga-té, Bodhi Svaha A: